CAN YOUR
RELATIONSHIP BE SAVED?

CAN YOUR RELATIONSHIP BE SAVED?

How to Know Whether to Stay or Go

DR. MICHAEL S. BRODER

Impact Publishers,® Inc.
ATASCADERO, CALIFORNIA

ATTENTION ORGANIZATIONS AND CORPORATIONS:
This book is available at quantity discounts on bulk purchases for educational, business, or sales promotional use. For further information, please contact Impact Publishers, P.O. Box 6016, Atascadero, CA 93423-6016, Phone: 1-800-246-7228. E-mail: sales@impactpublishers.com

---

Library of Congress Cataloging-in-Publication Data

Broder, Michael S.
    Can your relationship be saved? : how to know whether to stay or
      go / Michael S. Broder.
      p. cm.
    Includes bibliographical references and index.
    ISBN 1-886230-41-2 (alk. paper)
      1. Interpersonal relations. 2. Separation (Psychology) 3. Man-woman
    relationships. I.
    Title.

    HM1106 .B763 2002
    306.7--dc21   2002017215

Publisher's Note
This publication is designed to provide accurate and authoritative information in regard to the subject matter covered. It is sold with the understanding that the publisher is not engaged in rendering psychological, medical, or other professional services. If expert assistance or counselling is needed, the services of a competent professional should be sought.

Impact Publishers and colophon are registered trademarks of Impact Publishers, Inc.

Cover design by K.A. White Design, San Luis Obispo, California.
Printed in the United States of America on acid-free paper.
Published by **Impact 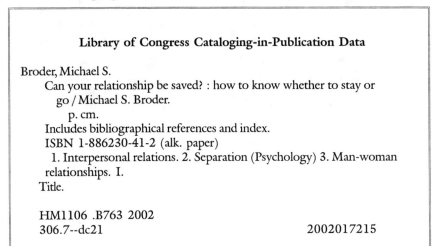 Publishers,® Inc.**
POST OFFICE BOX 6016
ATASCADERO, CALIFORNIA 93423-6016
www.impactpublishers.com

DEDICATION

~

To the Reader: *This book is dedicated to you and the rest of your life.*

CONTENTS

~

ACKNOWLEDGEMENTS

~

Let me take this opportunity to express my heartfelt gratitude to some of the people who made this book possible:

- To Bob Alberti, editor extraordinaire and publisher at Impact for his constant help and support in every aspect of bringing this book to fruition;
- To my wife and colleague Arlene Goldman for contributing her wisdom as well as the benefit of her many years of clinical experience which is generously reflected throughout this book;
- To my daughter and colleague Joanne Broder for never failing to provide living proof of the efficacy of single parenting, and for helping others professionally to benefit from her experience;
- To Sandra Brownell for her superb help in all aspects of preparing the manuscript;
- To Elaine Smith Esq. For her legal research and opinions, which appear throughout the book;
- And finally to the thousands of clients and couples I have seen over the years, as well as the many colleagues and others I interviewed for this book who shared with me so many of the real life scenarios, and invaluable insights that this book contains.

INTRODUCTION
HOW TO GET THE MOST OUT OF THIS BOOK

~

The title of this book, *Can Your Relationship Be Saved?* captures one of the most commonly explored issues that I have dealt with in my office over the past three decades as a practicing clinical psychologist. In addition to being so *common* a question, it has also been an extraordinarily *complex* one for scores of individuals and couples who have consulted with me over the years. Hopefully, this book will break it down in a way that you will find empowers you to quickly get beyond the murkiness, and toward a resolution of all the issues involved.

For the purpose of simplicity, I will use the term *relationship* throughout the book to refer to marriages, engagements, living-together and dating arrangements, or any other type of love relationship or romance — long- or short-term, and of any sexual orientation — including those where the partners are separated or divorced, thinking about reconciliation, or trying to justify leaving. I will use the word *partner* (present or ex) to mean spouse, spouse-equivalent, lover, mate, companion, boyfriend, or girlfriend.

This book is for you if:

- *You are in a troubled relationship* (such as one that has become stormy, passionless, indifferent or one-sided) and you are trying to decide whether to stay or leave; and what each possible direction would entail.

- *You are looking back at a relationship that has ended*, and find yourself second-guessing — by telling yourself things such as "if only I had _____ (fill in the blank) we would still be happily together" and find this to be a nagging source of discomfort.

- *You are trying to understand what went wrong in a relationship* that has ended (or is ending) so that you do not repeat old patterns.

- *You are trying to understand why the relationship of someone close to you* (such as a parent, adult child or other family member or friend) *might be ending* (perhaps even though it may have looked quite functional from the outside).

- *You are trying to understand your behavior or attitude patterns, or those of the people you become involved with.* Perhaps then you can come to grips with why your relationships either fail to continue, or don't seem to provide you with the fulfillment you are seeking.
- *You are exploring the issues this book addresses,* either by yourself *or* with your partner.
- *You are a mental health professional, clergyperson, attorney, or other helper,* who is in a position to help people make decisions related to their relationship transition, as well as to cope with the aftermath.

You Are Not Alone!

Since the late 1970s, our divorce rate has stayed at or around fifty percent. Statistically speaking, it is a fact that a woman coming of age during the first decade of the twenty-first century will, on average, have more husbands than children! Perhaps it is because we live so much longer in this modular society that major life changes (in careers as well as long-term relationships) are now so commonplace. I will leave it to others to judge whether this is a good or a bad thing. But what is most important is to *accept* this reality. For that reason, this book is written in a neutral tone. For example, rather than referring to an ended marriage as one that has *failed,* I will encourage you to acknowledge that a relationship has ended because *it ran its course.* In my talks, workshops, radio programs, and other writings, I have sometimes been criticized for my neutral attitude about this. But experience has convinced me that there is no such thing as a happy or *un*happy *couple* — only the happy or unhappy *people* (who constitute the couple). In addition, I have always believed that we are on shaky ground whenever we put our own values or judgments on what makes another person happy. *Remember, your happiness is way too subjective a matter for anyone but you to determine!*

This book will give you the right questions to ask in order to make the decisions you may now be facing, some direction in answering those questions for yourself, and the information and strategies you will need to help you to act on your decisions.

Ambivalence is a state of mind where you feel torn or stuck between one or more conflicting choices. Ambivalence results when you are unable to determine how you really feel about something. Ambivalence can be quite painful, and when you are in pain, you don't need glibness, clichés, pat answers or someone else's value judgments that will rarely hold up for you in the end. Instead, I will help you to honor the uniqueness of both you and your situation. This way you can resolve your *relationship ambivalence* with the confidence that you are going in the best possible direction and with all you need to meet the challenges that lie ahead — *all things considered*.

The Book Is Divided into Three Parts

• **Part I: Your Relationship** will focus on your relationship as it is now. In chapter 2, I will introduce a revised version of my *Can Your Relationship Be Saved?* self-assessment inventory that first appeared in my book, *The Art of Staying Together* (Hyperion, 1993). This self-assessment has been used by many thousands of psychotherapists, divorce lawyers, and lay people throughout the world. The feedback I have received on this self-assessment inventory since its inception has prompted me to revise some of the original items, and to add ten new ones. Based on your own evaluation of your relationship, you will be guided to chapters in the book that contain numerous and fresh strategies to help you look at each problem area.

• **Part II: Working Through the Curse of Ambivalence** has you evaluating the three major aspects of relationship ambivalence: 1) Staying versus leaving; 2) "What if I leave?" and 3) "What if I stay?" It is possible (and even quite normal) that you could be simultaneously identifying with all of these dilemmas (as well their subcategories). Therefore, I've included both strategies to resolve your relationship ambivalence and references to various other parts of the book that you'll find helpful.

• **Part III: The Aftermath of Ambivalence** will help you gain insight on both your new life together as a couple, *and/or* your life apart as someone who is once again single. You will have the opportunity to examine (or re-examine) each lifestyle, and to learn strategies that, if employed, will maximize your happiness *regardless of whether or not your relationship survives*.

How to Use This Book

Can Your Relationship Be Saved? is designed to give you the choice of reading straight through, or skipping right to your major area(s) of concern. However you choose to read it, *I urge you to utilize the strategies and exercises.* They will help you clarify the many issues presented as they apply to your own unique situation. You will find that the message in this book will have a different meaning for you each time you read or re-read various chapters; as you move along in your process, the message will evolve with you.

This book can help you develop perspective, so you'll know when you're heading in the right direction, given the reality of your relationship. You and I will collaborate to arrive at this perspective. I will provide the questions for you to ask yourself, and a litany of choices for you to consider along the way, together with some guidance as to how you can utilize your deepest internal sources — which is always where you'll find the best answers for living your life. No book could ever know what's right for you as well as you do, but together we will sort it out. And remember, while some of the things you read may really hit home, other points may not apply to you at all.

If you and your partner are *both* exploring the question of whether your relationship can be saved, I suggest that you each do the appropriate exercises and strategies separately and privately first. (You can then decide later what to share and what to keep private.) Many of them can be done in your head, while others should be written down and referred to often, as you progress through the book. Also, I recommend that you take your time with each chapter so that you can fully digest the material on an *emotional level*. What you will be reading is based on decades of clinical experience with countless individuals and couples representing practically every imaginable relationship situation and issue that you will need to consider.

Most importantly, this book is *about* you and the relationship that perhaps represents for you the most crucial aspect of your life. It deals with a serious and often frustrating *topic*, but in an upbeat and optimistic *manner*. So once again, I urge you to make maximum use of it by doing the exercises and making the most of those strategies that in any way speak to you. In this way, you will be able to integrate the material as thoroughly as possible, making the book more than just an interesting read. Then, you will be a lot clearer about your direction and next steps. In the Appendix at the end of the book, I list some additional resources for help — should you find yourself needing them.

Thus the main mission of *Can Your Relationship Be Saved?* is to help you to tap into the greatest resource you will ever have, to make this or any other major life decision — *your own inner wisdom*. I'm delighted to be a part of your process of growth, and I wish you success.

— Michael S. Broder, Ph.D.
Philadelphia, Pennsylvania

Part I:
YOUR RELATIONSHIP

~

This is a book about you and the rest of your life. It's also about choices and becoming empowered to make them. And it's about relationships — what it takes to make them work, when efforts to do so become futile, and where it's now best to take *yours* — if (and how) it can be saved and should be saved, or if it's too late.

Before we can know just where we are going, it's imperative to know where we are. In chapter 1, I'm going to ask you *a lot* of questions — very much like those I would ask if you were sitting with me face to face in my office. But these questions only need to be answered in the privacy of your own mind. Your answers will help you to evaluate the choices you will come to consider later in the book. All of my questions are designed to get you thinking clearly about your current situation and all of the options related to it.

Chapter 2 includes an inventory (yes, more questions!) that will help you do an even more thorough evaluation of your relationship. *The more we can work together on that comprehensive understanding of what brought your relationship to where it now is, the more meaningful you will find the information and strategies to be later on in resolving your specific situation.*

So consider Part I of the book to be a series of tools designed to stimulate you and get you ready to find the solutions you are seeking.

1

WHY DID YOU BUY THIS BOOK?

~

Here are just a few responses people gave when I asked why they would need this book:

- "To learn how to change *my partner* so that we can have a happy life together."
- "To see if there is any stone left unturned *before* leaving."
- "For the children."
- "To see how something that once felt so right *now* feels so wrong."
- "I just realized why I have been so angry and depressed lately, and now want to figure out what — *if anything* — I can do about it."
- "It doesn't feel like there's any more between us, but I cannot afford to leave, so maybe I can find a way to salvage our marriage."
- "I want children, my partner (whom I love) doesn't. It is crunch time and I need to decide whether to leave now in order to have the option of possibly getting this need fulfilled in some other way, or by someone else."
- "My partner *is not* a raging alcoholic, a child molester, or abusive in any way for that matter — yet *I am just not happy anymore.*"
- "We love each other but we're just not *in* love anymore."
- "I cannot stand the abuse any longer."
- "The kids have grown but we haven't. I feel chronically unfulfilled."
- "To see if there is a way to have a life — regardless of whether I stay or leave."

Could any of these statements have been made by you? If not, then how *would* you answer that question? However you would, read on.

Maybe you're feeling alone — or even odd — because you are pondering the direction you are going in your relationship? If so, let me assure you how normal *relationship ambivalence* has become! We all know that the divorce rate looms well over fifty percent. And that doesn't include people who live together and break up; people who are in long-term (non-live-in relationships); those who are in short-term relationships that can feel as emotionally intense as any marriage ever could; and those who *stay* in marriages and other long-term relationships which they describe as totally unsatisfying and unfulfilling. Add to that all those whose relationships have come very close to ending, for one reason or another, but have found a satisfactory resolution for both partners. Come to think of it, I can't imagine that there are very many of us who haven't been at this crossroad at some time, with one relationship or another.

Sometimes both partners in a relationship make the decision jointly about whether to continue or split. At other times, one partner makes it all alone. Indeed, if you were to ask me to make the one single most accurate statement regarding relationships it would have to be this: *For a relationship to begin — or to continue — there has to be a degree of desire, effort, or at least collaboration on the part of both partners; but for a relationship to end, all that is needed is for one partner to want it to end.* But as long as the door is open even a crack, it is, at the very least, theoretically possible to turn things around.

The Two Main Pillars of Relationships that Work

Before going any further, let's set up a frame of reference for looking at this issue. In my book, *The Art of Staying Together*, I highlighted what I believe are the two most important components of relationships that work: *passion* and *comfort*. Long-term relationships that serve the needs of both partners do so because they have an *acceptable degree of both passion and comfort*. Let's look at these two ingredients:

- *Passion* is all the romantic and sexual energy that gets you together as a couple in the first place. Passion is a great motivator. It prompts you to open your heart to someone, and is the stuff upon which longing, desire and certain types of intimacy are built. But passion *alone* cannot keep a relationship together.
- The second component is what I call *comfort*. Comfort is the ability to work things out, to enjoy each other's company, to respect each other, to share a common lifestyle, goals and values (financial, children, work schedules, etc.) and to live a peaceful and contented co-existence.

When it comes to making a commitment to each other, passion is the part of you that commits from the *heart*. However, it is your *brain* that determines whether your relationship provides you with a sufficient degree of comfort to warrant the commitment. Maintaining a sufficient degree of passion *and* comfort — for each of you — is really a lifelong job.

Troubled Relationships

There are three main categories of troubled relationships (which account not only for that alarmingly high divorce rate, but also the much higher percentage of significant non-married relationships which end). They include relationships that are *stormy*, that have become characterized by *indifference*, and those of a *one-sided* nature.

A *stormy* relationship is generally one that has plenty of passion, but not necessarily of the positive kind. Of course, positive passion is what we think of when we picture a relationship at its best. But when there's an excessive amount of *negative* passion of the variety seen in stormy relationships, the result is a tremendous amount of anger and *dis*comfort. At the extreme, these relationships can become abusive and even dangerous. A relationship with a lot of passion and little or no comfort can still be — and quite often (but not always) is — highly charged romantically and sexually. In some cases the most passionate sex actually occurs after the meanest and most volatile arguments. Sometimes anger even takes on the characteristics of "foreplay" for some of the best sex! This happens because after a nasty battle there's often an apology, which can temporarily *feel* as if the issue is resolved (which, of course it isn't). The act of making up then leads to tender, romantic and passionate feelings. Thus, negative passion turns into positive passion. The sad part is that the situation responsible for so much of the anger is never dealt with or resolved. Thus, the pattern can continue indefinitely. Ironically, most couples who follow this pattern often don't realize that the "reward" of sex as a resolution to the fight could actually be the reason why they fight so much!

The second category of troubled relationships is those that become *indifferent*. In this case, most — if not all — of the passion is missing. And although there can be a very comfortable living arrangement, partners may have little feeling or sexual desire for each other. Sometimes partners simply grow apart without anger, *or* there can even be as much anger present as there is in the typical stormy relationship. The main difference is that there's just not the tendency to argue or do battle with each other. This may be a result of the partner's personality styles, or the absence of passion altogether — including negative passion. Instead, the relationship merely begins to die a slow and quiet death. In other words, it may be *brain alive* but *heart dead*. (In contrast with a stormy, passionately driven relationship without sufficient comfort that is *heart alive,* but *brain dead*.)

Finally, there are *one-sided relationships.* In these cases one person usually puts out much more effort and energy toward the maintenance, nurturing and survival of the relationship than does the other one. In a one-sided relationship one partner can be quite content — having all the passion and comfort he or she needs — while the other partner feels somewhat to totally unfulfilled.

In all types of troubled relationships it is important to ask: "What is the potential for change?" If the answer is "none," the next question to ask yourself is, "Is this where I still want to be?"

What Are Your Problem Areas?

Now, let's explore *your* problem areas. What are the problems that now exist which have the potential to bring your relationship to an end? Reflect on your current relationship. *Make a list of the issues and problems, which now exist, that are prompting you to ponder if your relationship can be saved.* What are the issues and problems that have taken you to this point? When did they begin to become problematic? What may have initially precipitated the situation? Take a pen and paper out and list as many answers to these questions as possible. If you are not sure what to write down at this point, that is okay. In this and the following chapter I will be suggesting numerous ways for you to explore these often-difficult questions. But before giving you some of *my* ideas regarding what your problem areas are, take the time now (before turning to the next page) and make a record of how *you* see your relationship at this point. It will be helpful for you to refer to this initial list later on.

Potentially Threatening Problem Areas

See which, if any, of these you can identify with:
- Are you having an affair?
- Is your partner having an affair (or do you think so)?
- Has your sex life been disappointing? (For example, you are no longer sexually attracted to you partner.)

- Are you unable to communicate about important issues or areas of your relationship?
- Is there physical or emotional abuse?
- Is there an unusually thorny issue or ongoing problem (that you have been unable to resolve) that seems to be poisoning or undermining your total relationship or aspects of your relationship unrelated to that problem?
- Are either or both of you excessively or obsessively jealous?
- Have you lost trust for your partner?
- Have you lost respect for your partner?
- Has your relationship ceased to be a source of fun for you?
- Does your partner seem chronically unhappy with you in a way that you cannot satisfy him or her?
- Is there too much dependency or smothering in your relationship?
- Are there too many rules (that don't work for you) that you need to live by in order to make your *relationship* work?
- Do you experience your partner as rejecting you no matter what it is that you do?
- Did you have thoughts of calling it off the day of or the day before your wedding? (Perhaps you went through with the wedding only because it felt too late to call it off as opposed to reconnecting with your desire to marry).
- Have you and your partner lost (or never had) the ability to work out conflict?
- Have you and your partner been unable to adjust to a major change in your lives (such as the arrival of a new baby)?
- Is your partner insisting on a lifestyle change that is totally unacceptable to you?
- Is this relationship incompatible with pursuing what you see as your life purpose or next steps toward that purpose?
- Have you simply stopped growing together?
- Is there a drug or alcohol problem that looms over your relationship — mild to severe?

You may now wish to revise your "problem list" and include some of your answers to the above questions.

Then and Now

The title of a popular Off-Broadway play captures one of the most common sentiments I've seen: *I Love You, You're Perfect, Now Change.*

If you have discovered that perhaps you are no longer growing together, it can be useful to look at how you got together in the first place, and how your initial attraction to each other may have given way to a sense of frustration.

If a trait that *initially* attracted you to your partner was that of being:	You may *now* be seeing that trait as:
Eccentric	Crazy
Great sense of humor	Obnoxious
Take charge person	Control freak
Ambitious and successful	Workaholic and neglectful
Life of party	Excessive drinker
Someone who will take care of me	Not allowing me to take any initiative on my own
Relaxed and laid back	Lazy
Orderly and careful	Obsessive and compulsive
Risk taker/daring	Reckless/careless
Childlike	Childish
Intellectual and smart	Condescending
Self-aware/knows who he or she is	Narcissistic
Talented	Omnipotent
Sexy	Inappropriately flirtatious
Good parent	Too enmeshed with kids
Beautiful	Obsessed with looks
Very desirable	Can't be satisfied with me
Needs me	Too dependent
Sets high standards	Impossible to please
Fun	Can't be serious
Religious	Rigid rule abider
Spiritual	Self-absorbed
Careful	Paranoid
Vulnerable	Neurotic
Makes own rules	Sociopath
Strong ties with family and friends	Has time for everyone but me
Committed to a great cause	Unavailable
Tough	Unfeeling
Puts me in my place	Abusive
Determined	Ruthless
Nurturing	Smothering
Great money manager	Stingy
_____	_____
_____	_____

This illustrates how you could be seeing your partner very differently. You may now be irritated by traits that perhaps you initially found to be irresistible! In other words, there is a lot of truth to the cliché "be careful what you ask for." First impressions are important. Very often they are the beginning of the fantasies of what you expect from each other. When I ask people to share with me their first impressions of someone with whom they are having difficulties now, I often get what was predictably a preview of how the relationship is today:

• "When I first met him on that rainy day, he offered me his umbrella and was so kind. I had this great fantasy of him taking care of me, something that my ex never would do. But soon after we became involved, he started acting controlling, judgmental, and condescending toward me; he began to treat me as though I were inadequate."

• "My first husband was extremely hard-driven and unavailable. So I left him to hook up with my yoga instructor — someone who personified the exact opposite. But he turned out to be *so* laid back and *un*ambitious that I totally lost respect for him."

• "My first wife was so clingy and possessive that I often felt like I couldn't breathe. Then I met my present wife. She was extremely accomplished professionally. Her independence really turned me on. But she has now become so distant and aloof that I feel totally insignificant to her. *The funny thing is she really didn't change, only my perception of her did.*" (Great insight!)

• "My partner had some real problems related to her past that I recognized unmistakably when we were dating. But I really thought that our relationship and my love for her would smooth them out. What I found after we got married was that those dark sides even got darker."

When initial attraction is present, quite often the glass is half *full*. But when initial attraction leaves, that same "glass" becomes experienced as half *empty*. So consider some of these questions regarding how your relationship has evolved:

• If things have changed, was that change predictable (given a second look at those traits that initially attracted you)?

• Is it possible that things were always this way, but you didn't didn't notice (when looking through those "rose-colored initial attraction glasses")?

• Did you ignore the warnings? (Example: Your partner tells you she doesn't want children, or he has a hard time being monogamous.) Is it that you may not have heard certain clues?

• Did you fall for Mr./Ms. Right or Mr./Ms. *Right Now*? (In other words, were you very needy at the time when you hooked up? Perhaps in a rebound relationship where, in hindsight, you now recognize that your new partner at the time represented little more than a strong dose of "anesthesia" for the pain of a relationship you were ending?)

• Is it possible that you were never really attracted to your partner, but wanted the relationship for reasons other than attraction (or liked him or her so much that you were willing to overlook the attraction factor then), and now find it unacceptable that there is little or no sexual desire?

• Did you marry (or commit to a long-term relationship) because of who your partner *is* (this doesn't change very much), or because of what he or she can *do* for you (this does tend to change)?

• Why did you hook up (or get married) when you did? (See if you can get back into that frame of mind to see what you were thinking and feeling when the relationship was at its best.)

• Are there other factors that not only got you together, but also *kept* you together to this point that you may not be acknowledging?

• What are some of the important strengths of your relationship? (That is, what in your partner would you absolutely *not* want to change — even now?)

• Could a major part of the problem be *perfectionism*? (One man recently shared with me his wife's comments after she refused to go into counseling with him: "If we need counseling we should simply get divorced. Period!") Thus, is *any* imperfection — real or perceived — enough to make you or you partner question, negate, or even bolt the relationship?

After you have reflected on these questions, and maybe added some to your list of issues, you may want to go through them again — *only this time as your partner*, and take a look at them *as they apply to you. Warning: this can be a powerful eye-opening exercise.*

Continuing Your Relationship Assessment

As you continue to reflect upon where things are in your relationship now, here are a few additional questions designed to aid you in your understanding:

• What was your relationship like when it was at its *best*?

• When and how did things first change?

• How have you changed within the relationship?

• How has your partner changed within the context of the relationship?

• How would you describe your relationship at its *worst*?

• What have you tried to do to make it better?

• What has worked?

• What has not worked?

• What do you believe you *really* want now (as opposed to what you *should* want or would merely accept)?

• Are you still (even just sometimes) able to enjoy some of the activities together that made your relationship blossom at the beginning? Or have you simply let the fun and enjoyable activities you once shared go by the wayside (and then, perhaps, think of them as more of those *unpleasant realities* of day-to-day living)?

• How do you feel when you are *with* your partner? Do you like the person *you* are when you are with your partner, or has the relationship begun to bring out those parts of yourself that you like the least? If that is the case, does your self-esteem suffer when you are around your partner?

• Have you stopped growing both individually and as a couple in each other's presence? For example, are you still able to support and enhance each other in important areas of your lives? Or are the parts of your life that you feel best about those that tend to be disconnected from your partner?

• Has you partner done something you consider unforgivable, such as having an affair or lying to you about something really important?

• Do you see your partner as an unacceptable parent?

• Could you say that your relationship is one that was really destined to be only a *short-term* one (but is now disguised as — or mimicking — a mature, long-term relationship)? Or, to put it another way, was it good at the beginning when you had that great infatuation and effortless initial passion, but then did it simply go downhill from there? If so, is it possible that you mislabeled that infatuation (which generally decreases over time) as something more than it really was, such as love and intimacy (which is more likely to grow)?

• Has your partner squandered a lot of money you couldn't afford to lose? Become abusive? Done something else that has caused a blanket of anger to hide the positive feelings that were once there? (If this is the case then an important question to ponder as we go along is whether positive feelings or the potential for positive feelings still exist underneath that anger, or are they gone forever?)

• Besides the question of whether you *love* your partner, can you say that your partner is someone you truly *like*?

• What would have to happen for you to gain or re-gain respect? An acceptable degree of attraction? Trust? And even for you to be able to like your partner again?

• What would have to occur in order for your relationship now to become fulfilling to the point where you would no longer consider leaving?

• If you had to say goodbye now and end it, could you? If so, how would you do it?

• If you had it to do all over again, would you marry (or become committed to) you partner again?

Use the insights and reflections from these questions to add further to your list and to your awareness and understanding of where your relationship is *now*. Again, dare to reverse the roles and answer them as you imagine your partner's perceptions of you would be.

What Are Your Expectations?

Reflect on your *expectations* for your relationship. What are they? What is it that you really *want* from your partner? What *could* your partner do now that would — from your point of view — save the relationship? Make a comprehensive list, and pay special attention to what you now recognize your unique issues to be.

What Are Your Partner's Expectations?

If your *partner* were to compile a list such as the one you just did, what would he or she be asking of you? Compose a list of what you think your *partner's responses* would be, then take each of these answers *individually* and ask yourself what you would be willing to *give up*, *give in*, or *change* about yourself in order to accommodate your partner. What are you now willing to do (that you may not have been willing to do before) in order to save your relationship or to make the climate better?

Looking at Your Expectations

Many believe in a variation of the idea, "If only I had the right relationship, my life would be totally complete." But then once involved, the expectations become so high that in the end *no relationship* could possibly meet all of these expectations. Thus, it turns into an unfulfilling experience. *I've seen many relationships fall victim to the expectations put on them.* When this happens, it can be quite unfortunate. That's why it's important for you to identify and very carefully reflect on what your relationship expectations are. For example, perhaps you tell yourself that your partner should *always* "be there for you." Yet, when you look realistically at this request (or demand) you can see how tall an order that expectation can be. Can you *always* "be there" for your partner? Be clear about what it is that you *really* want and expect from your partner. What could your partner do *right now* that would make questioning whether the relationship can be saved *obsolete* or *irrelevant*? What would your *partner* say in answer to these questions?

By asking you to think about how *your partner* would respond to those same questions, I am pushing you to be *empathetic* (tuned in to what your partner feels, or your perception of it). Remember, that if you are working on these questions in private, there is no downside to allowing yourself to reflect on them with total honestly.

… And a Few Final Questions for this Chapter

- What does this relationship mean to you at this point?
- Is any degree of sexual desire still present?
- Are you staying around merely out of the fear of "going it alone"? For financial reasons? For the children? For social or religious reasons?
- Does the thought of giving up on your relationship trigger sadness, or bring a sense of freedom and relief? Do both reactions to splitting up — sadness and relief — come to the surface? Could it be that you're hanging in there merely because you are worried about what *other people* will think if you leave?
- Are you staying because you want to be part of a couple or in a relationship, even if your current partner is no longer the *person* you really want to be involved with?

These are some of the factors that I urge you to explore regardless of what stage your relationship at now in, how long you've been together, or what your level of commitment may be. The next chapter will take this process a step further, and offer some direction for addressing your issues.

2

CAN YOUR RELATIONSHIP BE SAVED? AN INVENTORY

~

If your relationship were *a fire,* is it still burning strongly? Flickering? Smoldering? Does it need kindling? A log? Or has the last spark of it *burned out* to the point where it's even too late for more oxygen? (After all, your relationship at one time had to be *on fire* in order for it to burn out.) Relationships that are characterized mainly (or solely) by passion are often, as songwriter Cole Porter put it, "too hot, not to cool down."

If it is more accurate to describe your relationship as one that is (or was) grounded in *comfort,* perhaps a better metaphor than fire is that of a business. And if so, do you need downsizing? Refinancing? New management? Or are you ready for bankruptcy court?

For over twenty years I have searched for a foolproof "litmus test" that could save people from the pain of fruitlessly trying to revive a relationship that has virtually no chance for success (as well as from abandoning troubled relationships that could be turned around if only the partners could see that proverbial forest for the trees).

Let me first give you the *bad* news. Whenever I thought I had it nailed down, a glaring exception to the rule would surface. Some of the worst relationships I have ever seen have survived, improved and even flourished! And some of those that seemed positively salvageable and loaded with potential have folded. Although there are good reasons for all of these exceptions, we only find them out after the fact — similar to the way a Wall Street session is reported on at the end of the day once the numbers are in. (Wouldn't it be great for our portfolios if that same degree of "wisdom" were available a few hours earlier?)

Now, before you get discouraged because I'm asking even *more* questions, let me give you the *good* news. The inventory that you are about to take in this chapter comes about as close to the standard of a litmus test as anything I have found. And the many colleagues of mine who have used it agree. I first put together the inventory — I call it "Can Your Relationship Be Saved?" — for my book, *The Art of Staying Together*. Since then, it has been used by scores of mental health professionals with their clients/patients — with good results. Over the years I have received tons of feedback, which I have taken into account to revise and expand the inventory. So think of it as a "heads-up" — to make you aware of some of the warning signs that exist, and to help you to see and to make the choices that lie ahead. Your self-assessment could lead either to the healing (and even deepening) of your relationship, or the straightforward decision to end it.

In chapter 1, I asked you to reflect upon a lot of "essay" questions; in this inventory they are of the "true/false" variety. I suggest (as I did in chapter 1) that you take this self-assessment by yourself. If it is appropriate, have your partner take it as well — *but separately*. If both of you take it, I urge you to wait until each of you is completely finished before you compare your answers or discuss any of the implications.

Please take a piece of paper and number it from one to fifty. Then simply put a check mark next to the number of each "true" statement that describes your relationship.

Can Your Relationship Be Saved? Self-Assessment Inventory

1. My partner and I no longer feel like friends.
   ___ True   ___ False

2. My partner and I have developed a very strong wall that separates us.
   ___ True   ___ False

3. I am constantly thinking about how nice it would be to have an affair.
   ___ True   ___ False

4. When my partner and I fight, it gets nasty and I am left with feelings of wanting to get out.
   ___ True   ___ False

5. My partner has told me at a time other than when we were in the middle of a fight that he or she would be happier if we split up.
   ___ True   ___ False

6. I am unwilling to accept my partner as he/she is. If this relationship is to continue, he/she will have to make some very major changes that he/she is unwilling to make.
___ True ___ False

7. My partner and I have little in common anymore.
___ True ___ False

8. I would leave this relationship in a heartbeat if I felt confident that I could make it on my own or if I knew I could get through the painful transition of a breakup.
___ True ___ False

9. Although I no longer love my partner, I feel responsible for him/her. I think the only thing that is really keeping me here is guilt.
___ True ___ False

10. My partner and I fight a lot and I fear that underneath the fighting there is not much left.
___ True ___ False

11. When I am about to be around my partner and I think of having to spend time with him/her, I get an empty feeling.
___ True ___ False

12. My partner and I are just no longer playing for the same team.
___ True ___ False

13. The more time goes by, the more I begin to dislike my partner.
___ True ___ False

14. My respect for my partner is practically or totally gone.
___ True ___ False

15. There is very little trust left in our relationship.
___ True ___ False

16. I constantly fear my partner's abusive behavior. If it happens again, I am leaving.
___ True ___ False

17. My partner abuses alcohol and/or drugs. It is even more intolerable to me that he/she denies that the usage is a problem.
___ True ___ False

18. I can only tolerate my partner if one of us is high on alcohol or drugs.
    ___ True ___ False

19. If I could afford it financially I would leave.
    ___ True ___ False

20. My partner has an emotional hold on me. I would love to leave but feel too hooked and addicted to the relationship.
    ___ True ___ False

21. My partner has children whom I am expected to relate to. The relationship would be fine if they were not there, but they are here to stay and it is creating a very unhappy situation for me.
    ___ True ___ False

22. I know I *should* want my relationship to continue (or *want* to want my relationship to continue), but I cannot say that I truly *do* want it to continue.
    ___ True ___ False

23. We are unable to resolve our differences together, but my partner refuses to enter counseling or therapy.
    ___ True ___ False

24. My partner has told me that he/she does not love me anymore.
    ___ True ___ False

25. My partner has done something for which I cannot forgive him/her. This was the straw that broke the camel's back.
    ___ True ___ False

26. We just have so many differences that it is unrealistic to think we can even begin to address them.
    ___ True ___ False

27. I am so overwhelmed by my partner's constant demands for love and approval, perfectionism, and/or rigid rules of how the relationship should be and how each of us should behave within it, that sometimes I just want to give up.
    ___ True ___ False

28. I am almost certain my partner is having an affair and if this is true I will not tolerate it.
    ___ True ___ False

29. I feel closer to my partner when we are not together.
___ True ___ False

30. There is definitely more pain than joy or pleasure associated with my partner and our relationship.
___ True ___ False

31. This relationship has become a constant burden.
___ True ___ False

32. If I knew I could find another mate, I would leave immediately.
___ True ___ False

33. I am having an affair with someone I value much more than my partner, and I am unwilling to give this other person up under any circumstances.
___ True ___ False

34. I feel very indifferent toward my partner and have little motivation to try and work things out.
___ True ___ False

35. My most stress-free moments are when my partner and I are not together.
___ True ___ False

36. My partner and I are totally inflexible with each other.
___ True ___ False

37. I don't even have a desire to tell my partner how I feel anymore — positive or negative.
___ True ___ False

38. Our relationship has peaked and could never again be as good as it once was.
___ True ___ False

39. When I think of us growing old together, life seems not worth living.
___ True ___ False

40. At this point, there is just too much water under the bridge.
___ True ___ False

41. When I think of leaving my partner I feel relieved.
___ True ___ False

42. I have wanted to leave for a long time, but my partner has said he/she will commit suicide if I do.
___ True ___ False

43. I constantly have to choose between my partner and my family (of origin).
___ True ___ False

44. My partner is abusive to the children — a situation I am powerless to stop as long as they are all in the same environment.
___ True ___ False

45. This relationship does not allow me to grow.
___ True ___ False

46. My partner does not fit into my future plans.
___ True ___ False

47. I want to leave but, I cannot see myself pulling it off — I am stuck.
___ True ___ False

48. I need my partner much more than I love him/her.
___ True ___ False

49. I love my partner but am not *in love* with him/her.
___ True ___ False

50. We have tried everything and nothing seems to help.
___ True ___ False

Evaluation of Inventory

Now let's take a look at your answers and what they mean. This self-assessment is a bit different from what you may have expected. Maybe you thought I was going to ask you to count the number of statements that were "true" (or "false"), and then based on that, I would give you a range of where you are *safe* to stay together, where your relationship is potentially in *trouble,* or where it is *doomed.* Don't be disappointed, but it's not all that simple! *Any one* of the items in this inventory to which you answered "true" could mean that your relationship is already in serious trouble to some degree — or heading there. In fact, this could be the only fifty-item test you will ever take where you could "flunk" on one item out of fifty!

What really needs to be looked at is the *reason* you answered "true" to any item where true applies — especially to those items that consistently characterize your relationship or which evoke negative emotions for you and/or your partner. Also, you may notice that some item or items apply to your relationship, but only to a mild degree (on a scale from zero to ten, say a "1," "2" or "3"). In this case, it may be accurate to consider the item in question to be a warning sign or signal that a serious problem could be developing, but you may have caught it in time.

What follows is another visit to each item in our "Can Your Relationship Be Saved?" Inventory. Only this time I have included the degree of risk an answer of "true" usually represents, some perspective on the item, and in many cases a reference to the chapter(s) of this book that contains strategies to explore that issue. Each chapter in Parts II and III is designed to be similar in nature to a "seminar" in the various topics, with many possible approaches to each issue covered, and strategies for solutions. *(Note: You will notice that I don't point you to specific techniques or strategies elsewhere in the book for each item in the inventory. This is because I want you to try them all. That is the only way you will quickly and precisely discover what works best for you in your own unique situation. Additionally, it's important to honor the complexity of your relationship by acknowledging that no one approach fits all. That's why this book contains so many strategies to choose from. However you may find it helpful to consult the table of contents for more help in locating a part of the book that most speaks to your individual items.)*

1. My partner and I no longer feel like friends.
    Moderate risk: Explore how this has changed over time, along with the following questions: Can you pinpoint the issue or issues that may be responsible? Do you want to be friends? What are you willing to do to turn this situation around? What could your partner do?

2. My partner and I have developed a very strong wall that separates us.
    Moderate to High-risk: What function is this wall serving? Would you really feel better off without it, or does the purpose it serves make you vested in keeping that wall standing? How troubling is your wall? Do you and your partner agree that it is a problem that deserves attention and a commitment to work through? If so, chapters 5 and 6 will be helpful.

3. I am constantly thinking about how nice it would be to have an affair.

Moderate risk: As long as it is kept on a fantasy level (unless your relationship is not a monogamous one). Is there someone in particular? Is your fantasy saying that your sex life is unfulfilling? Chapters 5 and 6 will contain some perspectives for addressing this issue.

4. When my partner and I fight, it gets nasty and I am often left with feelings of wanting to get out.

Moderate risk: This may indicate that the two of you need to learn to stay on the issue you are arguing about without allowing each disagreement to get *global* or *too personal*. That will enable you to fight more fairly. To address a climate characterized by anger, look at the *demands* and *un*realistic expectations that either or both of you may be putting on your relationship or each other. These demands are the backbone of that painful emotion of anger and the frustration that underlies it. The emotion of anger itself can take on a life of its own, and overwhelm — or become bigger than the issue or problem you are arguing about. Often when this happens and no relief is in sight, "getting out" can feel like the only *doable* option. In chapters 5 and 6, I offer some strategies for handling anger.

5. My partner has told me at a time other than when we were in the middle of a fight that he or she would be happier if we split up.

Moderate to High risk: When statements such as that are made in the heat of an argument, the problem is often one with anger itself. But when said at a relatively calm time, it could indicate that a rather serious high-risk problem — or problems — should be addressed. On the other hand, sometimes statements like that are the turning point. If a couple has avoided dealing with any unpleasantness, and finally starts talking about what may be an accumulation of a lot of small issues, they could resolve those issues one-by-one in order to clear the air (and then hopefully learn never to fall into that trap again). In that case, consider this a more moderate-risk item.

6. I am unwilling to accept my partner as he/she is. If this relationship is to continue, she/he will have to make some very major changes that he/she is unwilling to make.

High risk: The key word here is "unwilling." You are unwilling to accept your partner; your partner is unwilling to change. Something has to give — either your level of acceptance, your partner's attitude about changing, or your expectation of having a fulfilling relationship. In chapter 3, I will discuss the matter of breaking impasses.

7. My partner and I have little in common anymore.

Moderate risk: The most successful relationships are those that have commonality. But even the best couples do grow apart in certain aspects of their lives. So a discussion of what may be missing needs to occur. Then common interests, friends, or whatever it was you used to enjoy or share together needs to be revived in a way that makes sense given where you now are in your lives as a couple and in your individual growth processes. Chapter 6 will contain some strategies for developing more commonality together.

8. I would leave this relationship in a heartbeat if I felt confident that I could make it on my own or if I knew I could get through the painful transition of a breakup.

High risk: The culprit here could be your own self-esteem, and ability to see yourself as someone who can make it without a relationship, so that you are not wasting your life by staying together only out of fear and excessive dependency. Some strategies for arriving at this can be found in chapters 4 and 7.

9. Although I no longer love my partner, I feel responsible for him/her. I think the only thing that is really keeping me here is guilt.

High risk: Guilt can be a nasty set of "golden handcuffs," if that is truly all that's keeping you there. However, some people tell themselves this merely as a way of denying *their own* dependency. Chapters 4 and 7 contain some strategies for helping you to visualize a life outside of your relationship. See if this visualization makes a difference. Chapter 3 looks at the role of guilt in keeping relationships together.

10. My partner and I fight a lot, and I fear that underneath the fighting there is not much left.

Moderate to high risk: Anger often masks a lot of positive feelings that could be lying just beneath the surface. But to get to the good stuff, that anger has got to be resolved first. To the extent that the issues triggering your anger cannot be resolved (or you *confirm* that underneath there is not much left), this can become a high-risk item. Take some time when you are *not* feeling angry to identify and attempt to work as a team to resolve at least some of those anger-provoking issues you can both agree are there. Chapters 5 and 6 will give you some strategies to help you do this.

11. When I am about to be around my partner and I think of having to spend time with him/her, I get an empty feeling.

High risk: Often feelings of emptiness that are triggered in this manner indicate a longing for something that may not be able to be enjoyed while you remain in this relationship. Chapter 4 will help you look at this.

12. My partner and I are just no longer playing for the same team.

Moderate risk: Is this a mutual thing or just your feeling? Check this out. To the extent that it *is* a mutual thing, you can work together to resolve it. If your partner shares this concern, you may want to explore some of the strategies in chapters 5 and 6. If it is *not* mutual, explore what needs to happen *for you* in order to get back on board.

13. The more time goes by, the more I begin to dislike my partner.

High risk: This can result from the reality that you are not growing together, or that a resentment or disrespect is festering. The more this trend continues (without identifying and resolving the underlying issues), the more painful your life will become until the only option left is to separate.

14. My respect for my partner is practically or totally gone.

High risk: Restoring respect once it is gone is somewhere between extremely difficult and impossible. The only exception to the rule is if you can pinpoint a specific issue(s) that caused this trend to begin, and then work it through. Chapters 3, 5, and 6 contain strategies that are well worth your effort to explore if you are to save your relationship.

15. There is very little trust left in our relationship.

High risk: This is quite similar to item 14 in that lost trust that cannot be tied to a specific resolvable issue is usually irreversible. (An exception may be where the lack of trust is a personality staple that extends to many other aspects of life, such as in the case of people who characteristically tend to evaluate others in a paranoid manner.)

16. I constantly fear my partner's abusive behavior. If it happens again, I am leaving.

High risk: No one should ever have to tolerate abuse! "Waiting" for it to happen again is not an acceptable strategy either, unless some concrete steps have been taken to change this pattern. What is it that allows you to subject yourself to this? Do you think this type of behavior can ever be justified? Are you afraid of the repercussions of leaving? The practical issues such as money, the children, housing or further retribution? Or do you truly believe that something definitive can change? Just remember that experience has shown that *abuse does not usually extinguish itself.* Chapter 3 will help you to evaluate this while chapters 4 and 7 will afford you a look at what life for you could be if you choose to leave.

17. My partner abuses alcohol and/or drugs. It is even more intolerable to me that he/she denies that the usage is a problem.

High risk: Those who abuse alcohol or drugs or, better put, abuse *themselves* with alcohol or drugs, can make any relationship unworkable. Until the problem is acknowledged, you need to decide just how much of an issue this is for you and what your bottom line is with respect to your tolerance of it within your relationship.

18. I can only tolerate my partner if one of us is high on alcohol or drugs.

High risk: Many of the same reasons apply here that apply to item 17. The difference is that you need to be *anesthetized* in order to be able to stand your partner. Why? Is this something that you are unfairly laying on your partner? Or is the climate that intolerable? If the latter is true, at a time when you are sober look at every possible reason why this may be so. Strategies contained in all of the remaining chapters of this book can provide you help, depending on what issues you identify as needing to be resolved within yourself, with respect to your partner, and between the two of you — as a couple — for this to change. I realize that turning something like this around could be a tall order. But if you can't, the handwriting is on the wall.

19. If I could afford it financially I would leave.

Moderate risk: This is a very commonly heard mantra that many who have a feeling of generalized unhappiness believe until the opportunity to leave presents itself. Pretend for a minute you have no choice but to leave, and you *have* to make financial arrangements to do so. Chances are, if you had no choice you could pull it off. For example, many people who are rarely, if ever, bothered by the issue of financial security suddenly find themselves widows or widowers without life insurance or the other resources that would make it possible to continue their same standard of living. But somehow they manage to put their lives back together, even though they may (in better times) have doubted that they could. The only difference between you and those folks is that you have a choice, and they didn't! What you have in common is that you, too, will make it if only you can believe you will. Several strategies in chapters 3, 4, and 7 can help you with this vision. Remember the only resource that you cannot replace is time. And time spent in an unpeaceful, unhappy situation that you tell yourself you cannot change is perhaps the worst possible use of that irreplaceable time.

20. My partner has an emotional hold on me. I would love to leave but feel too hooked and addicted to the relationship.

High risk: What you are saying here is if you could become emotionally free, you would leave. Chapters 3, 4, and 7 will provide strategies to get beyond a situation such as this — or at the very least to see beyond it in order to make a choice.

21. My partner has children whom I am expected to relate to. The relationship would be fine if they were not there, but they are here to stay and it is creating a very unhappy situation for me.

Moderate to high risk: Blending families and step-parenting is an extremely complicated issue. Pulling it off requires maximum cooperation from both partners. You and your partner need to take this quite seriously and realize that you will probably not be together long unless you can maneuver this very difficult balancing act. On the other hand, if you are unwilling to work together, it is probably just a matter of time before this obstacle becomes too great for your relationship to overcome; thus you are at high risk.

22. I *should* want my relationship to continue (or *want* to want my relationship to continue), but I cannot say that I truly *do* want it to continue.

High risk: Chapters 3, 4, and 5 have much to say about this situation. Often that attitude occurs when passion has drained out of the relationship, but it still feels comfortable to stay. Experience shows that unless this is worked through, what comfort exists will drain away over time and lead to resentment.

23. We are unable to resolve our differences together, but my partner refuses to enter counseling or therapy.

Moderate risk: As widely accepted as counseling or therapy is to some people, to others there is still a stigma to it with lots of negative associations. I suggest that you find a therapist who works with both individuals and couples, and then initially attend yourself. If it is determined that couples therapy is indicated, work with that therapist on some strategies for bringing your partner in. Practically every therapist who works with both individuals and couples faces this situation routinely.

24. My partner has told me that he/she does not love me anymore.
Moderate to high risk: It is important to look at the context in which this statement was made. In the middle of an argument it is less serious, but nonetheless something that needs to be explored when the anger dies down. Without anger attached to it, it is more likely to be high risk. Chapters 3 and 5 contain some strategies to check out just what this means, as well as what the implications are.

25. My partner has done something for which I cannot forgive him/her. This was the straw that broke the camel's back.
High risk: The metaphor of the "straw that breaks a camel's back" indicates that there have been numerous unresolved issues that taken by themselves may be quite small, but when added up amount to something rather large. Learning how to deal with these (instead of sweeping them under the rug — to use another metaphor) is probably your only redeeming way to go. No relationship will survive happily if you can't learn how to get past life's upsets. Chapter 6 explores this in detail.

26. We just have so many differences that it is unrealistic to think we can even begin to address them.
Moderate risk: The question here is do you *want* to address them? Is this item true only when you are angry? Did these differences always exist? Are you only becoming aware of them now? Are they the flip side of some of the very reasons that you became attracted to each other, as discussed in chapter 1? Chapters 3, 5 and 6 contain strategies that can be helpful for evaluating just how much of a problem this may be.

27. I am so overwhelmed by my partner's constant demands for love and approval, perfectionism, and/or rigid rules of how the relationship should be and how each of us should behave within it that sometimes I just want to give up.
Moderate risk: What needs to happen for this climate change? Is this a constant thing or does it just come up only with specific issues? What compromises need to be made? What compromises can be made? Does your partner know how these things affect you? And is his or her attitude one of concern or indifference to your feelings? Numerous strategies throughout the remainder of this book will address different aspects of this issue.

28. I am almost certain my partner is having an affair, and if this is true, I will not tolerate it.

Moderate to high risk: Believe it or not, many relationships have become stronger after either the acknowledgment of an affair or the fear of it is brought out and dealt with. There is no easy answer here, because you are dealing with trust — one of the most important fabrics of the relationship itself. Chapter 3 contains ways to help you look at the issue of trust.

29. I feel closer to my partner when we are not together.

Moderate risk: This can just be a sign of burnout, which in a relationship is an indicator that perhaps you need to take some quality time for yourself. When you are ready to come back after a timeout, the relationship often will be much stronger. When I say, "time out" or "come back" I am not necessarily referring to a physical separation. It's possible that you need to examine some of your own goals and lifestyle options, including things that could or should be done apart from your relationship. Strategies to help you evaluate this situation are contained in chapters 3, 4, and 5.

30. There is definitely more pain than joy or pleasure associated with my partner and our relationship.

Moderate to high risk: If there is an *identifiable* issue causing this particular feeling, then this is a moderate risk item, and resolving that issue is your mission. This is often a temporary situation that can be gotten through. It becomes a high-risk item to the extent that there is *no* identifiable issue, but instead you are describing a more general feeling. So the first step here is certainly to identify what is making this statement true. Chapters 3, 4, and 5 could be particularly helpful to you.

31. This relationship has become a constant burden.

High risk: If this is the case, what is keeping you there? Even more importantly, can you identify what could possibly make you see the relationship more positively? Strategies in chapter 3 may help you to shed some light on this dilemma.

32. If I knew I could find another mate, I would leave immediately.

High risk: This all too common feeling is the one behind most rebound relationships. It is grounded in the notion that you cannot make it on your own. By discovering that you *could* go it alone, you are in a much better position to make the choices necessary here. Chapters 4 and 7 thoroughly address that.

33. I am having an affair with someone I value much more than my partner, and I am unwilling to give this other person up under any circumstances.

High risk: Based on nothing else but that statement, it is probably inevitable that should the person you are having an affair with become available as a primary relationship, that is the direction you will go. If this is not the case, then it's important to thoroughly explore just what it is that you are doing and why, so that at the very least this doesn't become a pattern you repeat in your next relationship. Strategies in chapter 4 will help you do that.

34. I feel very indifferent toward my partner, and have little motivation to try and work things out.

High risk: You are already out of the relationship *emotionally.* All that remains for you is the status quo. Is this acceptable? Only you can answer that. Chapters 3, 4, and 7 can be helpful to you here.

35. My most stress-free moments are when my partner and I are not together.

Moderate risk: Unless it goes beyond those specific issues that you recognize and are dealing with, and then it becomes *high risk.* How did the climate get to be this way? Does your partner also have this view of your relationship? Have you shared this feeling with your partner? Strategies for this item can be found in chapter 3.

36. My partner and I are totally inflexible with each other.

Moderate risk: Chances are you have unconsciously *collaborated* in your inflexibility. Again, does your partner share this view? Are you willing to discuss it, work on it and do whatever it takes to turn this pattern of inflexibility around? If you *both agree* that this is an important thing to do, you are most of the way there. Chapter 6 will give you helpful strategies. If there *cannot* be a mutual agreement to work on this, then nobody is winning. I would then direct you to chapter 3.

37. I don't even have a desire to tell my partner how I feel anymore — positive or negative.

Moderate to high risk: Depending on just what your hidden feelings are, this could be a high-risk item. What has made the idea of sharing your feelings so distasteful? Has your partner shown an unwillingness to hear what you have to say? Do you fear consequences such as rejection? It sounds as though your long-term happiness, both individually and as a couple, depends on taking the risk. Once you are able to at least try to communicate, I think things will become much clearer to you. However, if what you are saying is that the relationship is so dead that it is not even worth the effort, then you are in extremely high-risk territory. In this case, you need to ask yourself why you are procrastinating with what is probably the inevitable.

38. Our relationship has peaked and could never again be as good as it once was.

Low risk: Many couples believe that their relationship is on the way down when that effortless initial passion begins to wear off. But the real issue here is acknowledging together the desire for what you had, and working as a team to recreate it. This is a normal adjustment issue (not unlike having children or relocating) that can *feel* far worse than it really is in terms of the stress it might potentially put on to you as a couple. Your willingness to see it for what it is and commit to getting past it together is usually most of the battle. (However, a lack of that willingness from either partner to do what it takes to get past your adjustment issues together certainly has the potential to upgrade them to moderate or even high risk!) This is the only item in this inventory that is actually low risk because it is something that virtually every couple experiences in one form or another throughout the course of a long-term relationship. (In fact, my definition of a long-term relationship is one that survives the normal bumps in the road such as the decrease of that initial passion.) Unfortunately, many couples put far more weight on this feeling alone than it usually deserves!

39. When I think of us growing old together, life seems not worth living.

High risk: With this feeling, what could possibly be keeping you there? *Please* explore this thoroughly with the strategies in chapter 3 and 4 and then 7.

40. At this point, there is just too much water under the bridge.

Moderate to high risk: This implies an accumulation of issues (often the small ones you have hoped would go away by ignoring them) that have not been dealt with as they have come up (similar to that "straw" that always seems to break the camel's back). If you still harbor a desire to keep the relationship together, start by looking at those issues one-by-one until the answer becomes clear. If there is no desire to do that, then upgrade this item to high risk.

41. When I think of leaving my partner I feel relieved.

High risk: It sounds as though you are beginning to accept the inevitable. Chapter 7 will be especially helpful to you.

42. I have wanted to leave for a long time, but my partner has said he/she will commit suicide if I do.

High risk: You need to weigh the rest of your life against this threat. There are no easy answers here. But as long as a threat of this type is the only thing keeping you together, what hope is there for you to have any fulfillment? Any threat of suicide must be taken seriously. Thus, as a most important short-term issue, your partner and his or her state of mind certainly need to be attended to. But *your* long-term happiness does not deserve to be neglected or ignored either. There are strategies for you in each remaining chapter in the book.

43. I constantly have to choose between my partner and my family (of origin).

Moderate risk: Both your partner and your family are realities that cannot be ignored. The first question you might ask yourself is whether you are willing to do whatever it takes to reconcile the differences and/or work out a peaceful arrangement where you can all coexist. If not, then you know that a difficult choice — where somebody will not be happy — will inevitably need to be made.

44. My partner is abusive to the children — a situation I am powerless to stop as long as they are all living in the same environment.

High risk: This is one situation where you have to look at what your highest duty is. Legally, morally, and ethically, a "true" response to this statement says that *you need to leave* — if not for your own peace of mind, for the protection of your children. This is one item where there is very little flexibility — if any — or room for margin of error.

45. This relationship does not allow me to grow.

Moderate to high-risk: Couples in long-term relationships — particularly those that began when the partners were young — often find that as individuals they have slowly begun to walk on different paths. When this happens — if enough passion and comfort are still present, and there are feelings and a desire on both of your parts to stay together, you can work on changing the climate so that your personal growth *is* possible. However, this item will become high risk to the extent that either of you is inflexible about making the kind of changes that will allow both of you to grow as you need to.

46. My partner does not fit into my future plans.

High risk: This sounds like a very unambiguous statement. Can you come to any basis for keeping the relationship intact? If this cannot be converted to a relationship issue where both of you are willing to make some necessary and crucial changes, there is not much that can be done.

47. I want to leave, but I cannot see myself pulling it off — I am stuck.

High risk: Your desire to leave is pretty straightforward. But what is the glue that still keeps you there: The children? Change in social status? Finances? Family rejection? Feelings of failure or inadequacy? Fear of going it alone or not meeting someone else? Perhaps you are someone who puts down divorced people, never expecting yourself to be in that category. Do you fear your own future? (These are just a few of the possible reasons behind this statement.) It's important now for you to soul search and see exactly what is behind your saying "I cannot." That is the key. When strategies to deal with each of them are explored, see if there is still resistance. If so, then chances are you are not being honest with yourself regarding your desires. Look for hidden issues. Strategies in chapter 3 should be helpful to you in this regard.

48. I need my partner much more than I love him/her.

Moderate risk: Many stay in relationships out of need. That is a decision regarding values that only you can make. There are ways to rekindle what sparks are left. (See chapter 6 for strategies.) But try this exercise: Make a list of what the needs are that your relationship fulfills. For each need you list, try to identify an alternative method of fulfilling it. Do this in the privacy of your own mind. See if or how this exercise changes your perspective. Also, consult the strategies in chapter 5.

49. I love my partner but am not in love with him/her.

Moderate risk: This is the passion versus comfort dilemma. *Truly* loving a person is usually incentive to leave no stone unturned in trying to arrive at a satisfactory degree of fulfillment. You could be harboring some romanticized (as opposed to romantic) notion that solid relationships don't need to be worked on. Most classical love stories are about short-term relationships, where the book or movie ends before the lovers' initial passion does. Strategies in chapters 5 and 6 for re-igniting passion, along with a frank and intimate discussion about your feelings, could make the huge difference here that you are seeking.

50. We have tried everything and nothing seems to help.

Moderate risk: Hopefully in the remaining chapters of this book you will find numerous strategies that you haven't tried. If this item is still true by the time you complete this book, take a good look at what is really keeping you together. Your bond may be a lot stronger than you think.

How to Make the Most of this Inventory

Most of the *moderate risk* items refer to issues which can actually be resolved — as difficult as they may be — provided, of course, you and your partner are willing to work hard in the direction of resolving them with the intention of staying together. *High risk* items on the other hand are those most correlated with relationships that cannot be saved unless a full and mutual acknowledgment of these serious issues, along with major and generally difficult changes by both of you, are made.

To summarize, for each item you answered "true," can you pinpoint the problem areas that brought you this far? Theoretically, what would have to happen for your relationship to get better, or the very least, to be working again? Are you willing to make those necessary changes that are important if your relationship is to stay intact? Is your partner willing? At the very least are you willing to thoroughly discuss the items for which you answered "true" and your feelings about them with your partner? What are you willing to do to demonstrate that flexibility? If changes by either of you are not on the horizon, is it possible to learn to accept things the way they are?

Consult the list you began in chapter 1 and add to it the additional issues you have identified (or become aware of) by taking this inventory. *If you knew that your relationship would never get better, what would be your next step?* What are the minimum criteria for determining what "better" or "salvageable" is? What are your partner's? Are you both willing to talk about this? These are some of the important things for you now to explore. The chapters in parts II and III of this book will help you to do that.

PART II

WORKING THROUGH THE CURSE
OF AMBIVALENCE

~

To the extent that you've identified the issues that *underlie* your relationship ambivalence, you have probably noticed one of two things: Either (a) the direction your life will now take — staying versus ending your relationship — is an obvious one (in which case Parts II and III will further clarify the steps that you realize now must be taken), or (b) there is even more confusion than you may have imagined. In the latter case, Part II will help you to sort through your confusion and hopefully put you on track for a resolution to this most complex dilemma. All of the combinations are here for you to examine. *Numerous strategies are provided for you to explore leaving, staying, and your ambivalence itself.*

Because there are no pat answers, the journey to resolving ambivalence will be different for each person who reads this book, and for you, each time things change in your life externally or within yourself. Therefore, I urge you to try each of the strategies that could — in any way, shape, or form — apply to your situation. You may experience the results of some as home runs — *incredible feelings of clarity*. Some strategies may take you to places that seem too obvious, while others will have little or no relevance to your situation at all. But keep in mind that all of the strategies I have included in this book are proven in clinical practice. Many of them, as you will see, can be quite powerful.

So feel free to experiment. And remember that you can expect success only to the extent you will commit to making the *changes* that can resolve your ambivalence. It is not unusual to have to repeat a strategy many times, before it fully delivers. But if you persist, it will. Your commitment to doing whatever it takes to bring about the clarity and the changes you are seeking, is the most important ingredient to your journey!

By the time you've completed the chapters and exercises in Part II, I'm confident you will be feeling quite ready to put your ambivalence behind you!

3

THE PAIN OF STAYING
VERSUS THE PAIN OF LEAVING

~

It has been said, "confusion masks the obvious." After assessing your relationship in chapters 1 and 2, again, you may notice that you are even more confused than you were before. In this chapter we will explore why that may be, and consider some strategies for addressing your confusion — which has the potential for making any important decision feel quite fuzzy, and even painful. The type of confusion that renders you unable to make a decision (no matter how straightforward that decision may seem to other people, or even to you at times) is called *ambivalence*. (Examples of relationship ambivalence include: wanting to leave, but not wanting to let go of the parts of your relationship or lifestyle you do value; being torn between the good parts of both your relationship and what you perceive as your life after the relationship ends; wanting to stay, but feeling intolerant of certain aspects of your relationship; or being unhappy with your relationship, while scared of what awaits you if you leave it.)

What Is Ambivalence?
Ambivalence is a feeling that we all have experienced at one time or another in some important aspect of our lives. But if you are ambivalent in a lot of areas of your life, consider this: *Ambivalence in and of itself can actually destroy your life!* That's right! Theoretically, if you had everything you could possibly want going for you, but were ambivalent about the decisions you make — particularly with respect to your life direction — no matter what you did have going for you, no matter what you choose to do, you could be dwelling on the fact that you should be doing *something else.* That is the trait of ambivalence. And no matter what kind of life you have made for yourself, being ambivalent about it could ruin the quality of it all. So before going any further, let's look at that trait of ambivalence itself.

First, let's acknowledge that we all have at least some degree of ambivalence. Since life itself is such an extremely complex process, and certain aspects of our lives often get more complicated as they evolve, a certain amount of ambivalence is actually normal. In fact, a tiny amount of ambivalence might even serve to protect you sometimes from being thoughtless about certain decisions and steps that need to be reasoned out carefully. But the problem comes in to the degree that you allow yourself to operate under this all-too-common myth: that there is one and only one absolutely right answer that will contain no shades of gray. The myth continues when you believe that by being indecisive and holding out long enough, some certain, indisputable and absolute answer will somehow come to you. And when it does — you believe — it comes with an ironclad guarantee that you will *never* have any regrets, nor will you ever second-guess those decisions you do make. Since this standard is so incredibly high (not to mention black and white), it then follows that *you will resist making tough decisions at all that you are the least bit ambivalent about!*

By remaining ambivalent, you are making a decision by default — that is deciding by making no decision. That could mean remaining in what I have long called "a comfortable state of discomfort" (in this case, comfortable with the status quo, but uncomfortable with your relationship). By taking no action, you resist going in any direction that contains a shade of gray, even if that direction might ultimately lead to a solution for your problem. And what important life issue doesn't contain some degree of uncertainty? *Certainly not the area of relationships!*

Some people actually have a fear of making decisions altogether. If that's you, it is likely you have many regrets about things that may have passed you by, simply because you didn't act decisively when you had the opportunity to do so. If you think my statement that "ambivalence can ruin your life" is a little too strong, perhaps you may even take comfort in the ambivalence. But my stand on ambivalence is rather *unambivalent: to the extent that ambivalence exceeds prudent caution it will generally serve to hold you back;* and that can be any area of your life (relationships, career, family and business matters or lifestyle choices). So if you are feeling ambivalent about your relationship right now, consider your ambivalence to be as worthy of resolution as any of your other relationship issues. Then you can look ambivalence squarely in the eye. Here are a few ways to attack ambivalence:

• *Remember that just about all of your important decisions are, to one extent or another, educated guesses.* And most of these important decisions have factors that would pull you in the opposite direction. After all, a decision without conflicting factors — to one degree or another — would be a no-brainer. There is nothing "no-brainerish" about whether and how to work toward continuing or ending your relationship!

• *Forget about certainty.* The concept of certainty itself is a myth. Instead, *believe in yourself.* Hindsight — as we all know by the cliché (at least intellectually) is 20/20. There are many things every one of us would do differently "if only we knew then what we know now." But that's never an option, so stop pretending it is! Where you do have unlimited power (even if at times you are not in touch with it) is in making changes that will affect you from today on, and for the rest of your life — beginning right now. By focusing on that you can start looking upon decisions not as horrible burdens, but as challenges. (It has been said to me many times, and in numerous ways, that the "luckier" ones are those for whom the decision has been made by their partners.)

Think of some significant or important life choices you have made in the past — recently or even a long time ago — of which you are most proud. Make a list of them and continue to expand your list. Be sure to include those choices that may have led to major life changes. Keep this list as a frame of reference that you can refer to for a shot of empowerment anytime you find yourself thinking that you are incapable of rising above your ambivalence.

Now let's get back to your relationship.

If You Are Questioning Whether to Stay or Go
For many years now I've been happily in my second marriage. But when I was going through my own first marriage separation and divorce in the early 1970s, I took great issue with the idea that my first marriage had been a failure. Indeed it yielded a wonderful child; and undoubtedly it was a source of great pleasure for a significant period of time. And as a dividend, there was quite a bit of learning and personal growth. I certainly did not feel like a failure, and I refused to write off the entire five-year marriage as one that never should have occurred! True, my first marriage failed to continue, but so do many meaningful experiences in life.

So after a lot of thought, I arrived at the explanation I referred to in the introduction to this book, which I consider to be much better. It is one that helped me to put the experience into perspective, as it has for the countless people I have seen in my practice, spoken with on the radio, and met at my talks and seminars. It's the idea that

> *relationships that end do so not out of failure, but merely because they have run their course.*

Perhaps you have seen other important elements of your life run their course, such as a job, a career, or a lifestyle you once cherished. Perhaps they did not seem to fit as you got older and/or as your life (as well as the lives of those around you) changed. Think about your family of origin. If you left home, does that mean your family relationships failed? It probably does not (at least not just because you left home). More accurately, *that time of your life was simply over.* It ran its natural course, and it was time to move on. Though the transition may have been a difficult one (and most life transitions — even the happy ones — have their periods of difficulty), it does not mean that you regret it.

Time to Go? If after taking the self-assessment inventory you have determined that *your relationship has run its course,* chances are you will find much of what is discussed in the pages that follow to be helpful to you in the transition. Here are some strategies you can employ right now toward that direction:

• *Determine the practical and logistical steps in ending your relationship, and then make a preliminary to-do list for the major life change that lies before you.* I suggest this because to many, leaving a relationship feels like a task that is extraordinarily overwhelming. By breaking it down into a series of manageable and actionable items, then into sub-tasks and sub-sub-tasks, you have made it into a doable project that is less intimidating and far less subject to procrastination. Your list can include such things as finding an apartment, consulting an attorney (and perhaps a financial consultant), raising (saving, borrowing, liquidating assets, etc.) the money you will need, telling your partner about your decision (as well as your children, family members and friends) and everything else than needs to happen in order to set your transition in motion.

• *For each of your to-do list items, give special thought as to how you can accomplish each task in the best possible way, without creating more pain or more obstacles for you or anyone else involved.* Remember, you are still at the planning stage. This means you can consider what you are now thinking about to be private. There is nothing that *needs* to be shared with anyone else at this point. *Only one caution: pay particular attention to the issues of young children who are often more vulnerable during this period.*

• *Make a list of what sources of support you may need at this point in order to help you get through your emotional issues* (such as your guilt, your anger, your fears and anxieties, your loneliness or isolation) regarding the breakup.

Chapters 4 and 7 will contain additional strategies and perspectives for handling your emotional issues.

Or Worth Staying? However, if you are still hopeful about *saving* your relationship, consider this: *if both of you are willing to work — by whatever means — on the most serious issues, your relationship is still viable!* In the self-evaluation, you had the opportunity both to define what these issues are, and to consider whether they spelled high or moderate risk. Here are some questions you (and perhaps your partner) need to be asking yourselves at this point:

• Can you pinpoint the *problem areas* that brought you this far? If you and your partner can at least agree on the nature or categories of your issues and problems, you are taking a significant step in the right direction.

• *What would have to happen* for your relationship to become fully viable once again?

• *Is your partner willing (or unwilling) to make certain changes* which are important to the prospect of your staying together? *Are you yourself willing?*

• *Are there things that you and your partner can do together* to give your relationship another life?

• Are either of you being *inflexible* at this point?

• If your partner is the only one who is being inflexible, what are you willing to do to *demonstrate your flexibility?*

• If changes by neither of you are on the horizon, is it possible to learn to *accept things the way they are?*

• If this acceptance is the *only* major sacrifice you would have to make, are you willing to do it for the sake of saving your relationship?

• What exactly does your relationship *mean to you at* this point?

• What is it that you *really do need* from your partner?

• What is it that you are *willing to give* your partner in return? (You may want to consult the list you started in chapter 1, and add to it in order to reflect the additional issues which may have since come up for you.)

• If your relationship *never gets better,* what would be your *next step?* What are your minimum criteria for determining that your relationship is salvageable? And what are your partner's? (Have you talked about this and, even more importantly, are you willing to talk about it now?)

• Are you insisting that your partner *be something that he or she is not?* (Examples: Your best friend? Someone toward whom you can feel more sensual? Share more intimacies? Be more trusting of? Someone with whom you can merely lead a peaceful co-existence?)

• *What are the specific steps* that either or both of you have to make in order for the changes to come about that are needed to save your relationship?

• *Picture yourself making those changes* you have identified. What would your relationship then be like? Would you now be out of the woods?

Or "Toughing It Out"? If you are holding an unworkable relationship together, think about why that is so.

• Is it for the *kids*?

• Is it for *financial reasons*?

• Is it out of *guilt* for what will happen to your partner if you make the unilateral decision to leave?

• If you had *no ties other than your emotional attachment* to your partner (in other words, if you had no limitations or external reasons to stay in your relationship — such as finances or children), would you stay or would you leave?

These questions obviously have no "right" or pat answers. Although many people I have encountered throughout my career have asked *me* for one, there is no universal standard regarding how much someone should or can tolerate or expect from a partner! Indeed, everyone's threshold or tolerance for pain and definition of life quality is different. Thus, all of the questions are designed for you and your partner to discuss together (if appropriate) — but certainly for each of you to think about and weigh separately — based on the issues you have identified. However, this chapter will help you to explore *your bottom line*, which is the only "right" answer you should ever trust!

Here is a handy way to check out your bottom line (and perhaps even your partner's) as you take advantage of the perspectives this book offers you. On a scale from zero to ten, with "0" being not at all, "1" the weakest, and a "10" being the strongest, how much do you want your relationship to continue? Answer this question with a number. A "0" means you unambivalently do not want the relationship to continue; a "10" means you have no doubt at all that you do want it to continue. Consider this strategy to be a snapshot you can always use, but one that is subject to change at any point in time for a variety of reasons. If you and your partner have numbers that are very far apart (For example, if you're an "8" and your partner a "3," that can explain much about your difference in motivation to work things out.) If you both are at "2" or both at "9," that can obviously be quite helpful to know as well. In my office, I routinely ask for a number from each partner (with the other partner out of the room) at the very beginning of couples' therapy. Then I will check on how (or if) the number changes periodically. If appropriate in your case, you and your partner can even have a great discussion about how you can work together to bring each of your numbers to "10."

Now let's see what some others have found to be the defining moment in their decision to stay or leave.

The Crunch Point

A "crunch point" is where your period of ambivalence is over and a decision is made. And although second-guessing is always an option (wouldn't it be nice if it weren't?), once the crunch point is reached there is no turning back. Let's look at what several people have found to be the situation or realization that brought them to this level of clarity. For this first group, the decision was to *leave.*

• "I realized that this relationship was damaging me. *I couldn't grow*. It finally dawned on me that to stay would mean a lifetime of depression."

• "I had to face the fact that we were just *no longer emotionally connected* and there was no way to reverse this."

• "First we became completely detached sexually — I had no sexual desire at all. Then, I realized that we began to avoid each other altogether. Finally, the desire to do anything about it went out the window as well. *There is nothing left.*"

• "I *stopped liking myself* for staying."

• "I realized that I am *only staying for financial security* and this is simply not enough."

• "I realized that when you take away the intense sexual passion we had for each other, *we didn't really like each other very much.*"

• "We were opposites in many ways. At the beginning this wasn't a problem, but then it became apparent that *we did not have the desire* (nor the capability) for doing the hard work necessary to resolve our issues together."

- "I *refused to be abused any longer,* and could no longer believe the promises that it will stop."
- "There is *no love here* and it's not because I'm not lovable — I know better."
- "We *can't talk about anything meaningful without fighting*. We've been in couples' counseling four times and it hasn't helped."
- "My partner is totally unavailable when high or drunk and refuses to change. *In reality I've been alone for quite awhile*. Now I have to take control of my life before it's too late."
- "My partner had an affair. I keep hearing that I should forgive, but *I can't forgive*, I don't even want to try. I want out."
- "It simply wasn't working, and hadn't for a long time. *Somebody had to leave*. One day, I simply went from, 'why me?' to 'why *not* me?'"

These people ended their states of ambivalence with the decision to *stay*:
- "I realized that I had to stop expecting my partner to magically know what I wanted. *As soon as I learned to ask for what I wanted* (rather than expecting it automatically), our relationship started to work again."
- "I stopped thinking of everything in terms of me and started *thinking in terms of us*. My partner reciprocated, and everything changed as a result."
- "We'd started talking about splitting. Then something incredible happened. For the first time *we started really talking*. In the process we've become way more intimate. Now neither of us wants to leave. Our crisis was a real blessing in disguise!"
- "We weren't feeling sexual toward each other and thought that our relationship was over. Then *we talked about some issues* that had been bothering each of us for a long time. It wasn't until then that we discovered what real intimacy was."
- "*My partner's affair was a wake-up call*. I never thought we would survive it, but this crisis made us able to see what our issues were. Now our relationship is stronger than ever."
- "I kept telling myself that I was only staying for the children and to preserve the status quo. But then I realized the problem was that *my expectations were too high*. By no longer expecting everything to be perfect, I no longer entertain the idea of leaving."

• "We were at the brink of separation. We had neglected our relationship for a long time. But the thought of *the impact on our children* as well as to ourselves made us reverse course to make working things out a number one priority. Guess what? We pulled it off! And in doing so, we went from blaming our children for having to stay together, to crediting them with providing us the motivation to turn things around."

• "We never knew how to fight fairly. There was so much anger in our relationship that I couldn't see the forest for the trees and wanted to get out. But by *simply learning how to handle anger and not take things so personally*, our marriage has gotten a whole new life."

Perhaps you can identify with one or more of those crunch point statements above — in either or both directions! Or perhaps you are now beginning to formulate one of your own.

Each of the following couples demonstrates the complexity of this dilemma:

∼

Dan and Jennifer had an extremely intensive whirlwind romance. Jennifer described it "like a great gourmet meal, but where you get food poisoning as a result." What she meant was that for her the passion and intensity were positively overwhelming. Both used words like "delicious," "engaging," "intense." But outside of this extreme passion and romance, the relationship could not work. Jennifer was turned off by what she described as "Dan's lack of ambition." Dan felt that Jennifer was "way too demanding and rejecting of who he was." By accepting the fact that this relationship probably was not one that would continue in the long-term, they each gave to themselves permission to enjoy the good things and not demand anything else. Their relationship continued for a few more months, and then simply fizzled out. In this case, by merely adjusting their expectations they could be at peace with the reality of the situation (which they mutually agreed on). When that effortless initial passion leaves, there can still be a good bit of sexual passion. But without the elements of comfort (in addition to the passion), the relationship may be extremely volatile. Many couples in a scenario similar to this decide that they will do whatever it takes to establish those "non-passionate" traits together (along with the ability to work out their issues and to give each other acceptance, etc.). A relationship may be quite volatile, but merely a strong commitment to establish that necessary pillar of comfort can make the vital difference.

～

Janice and Steven lived together for several years with the stated intention of getting married "when the time was right." For Janice there was urgency. Steven was consistently putting it off. Finally, Steven proposed. That's when Janice discovered that marriage to Steven was *not* what she wanted. Janice later described it, as a case of "be careful what you wish for." After exploring this turn of events, the couple amicably decided to split. In this situation, each later acknowledged that by splitting when they did, they saved themselves the legal and financial hassle of a divorce later on. The potential of their relationship obviously turned out not to be what they originally hoped it would.

～

Art met Cathy right after his separation. They got very involved very quickly. Both initially thought that the relationship would last. But Art became increasingly distant after several months. Then just as quickly, they drifted apart. This was a *rebound relationship*. And like most rebound relationships — although there can be an extraordinary degree of attraction and can *feel* like "the real thing" — they are often paramount to that dose of "anesthesia" necessary to get you through the pain of your previous relationship. But like anesthesia, rebound relationships can also have side effects. And when the pain it was designed to help conquer subsides, often the need for that rebound relationship does as well.

～

Mary and Seth were both thirty-four years old and had been married for ten years when Seth confessed to Mary that he had just terminated an affair with another woman. Although Seth had clearly come back to Mary and wanted to come clean about things, Mary began to panic about whether she wanted to stay with Seth. She feared that he would do it again. Her other fear was that she would stay with him until it was too late for her to have children and then affirm her fear that she couldn't trust him. They were able to stay together only by realizing that they had opened a brand new channel of communication. At the same time, however, she acknowledged that there were no guarantees their reconciliation would be permanent. That is a reality in any relationship! This case illustrates that some issues may not break you up, but they might *wake you up*. Five years later Mary and Seth credit this crisis in making their relationship stronger.

∼

Paul and Barbara, on the other hand, had periods of relative peace in their twenty-four-year marriage, in between crises (an affair, some major and distancing disagreements about family issues, and a financial crisis where Barbara gave a family member a sizeable sum of money without consulting Paul). In their case, each crisis would lead to a temporary resolution where they would make up until the next time. The problem is nothing would get resolved in a way that would provide insight to help avert the next crisis. Following a nasty series of arguments, they split. It was Barbara's decision, but Paul gave little resistance. This case demonstrates the proverbial rubber band metaphor where you can stretch a rubber band to a certain point and it keeps coming back, but take it one millimeter too far, and it snaps in two (in a relationship this means making reconciliation impossible). Also, because Paul and Barb tended to reconcile without resolving the issue (merely as a way to end the pain of their immediate crisis), nothing except that immediate pain was resolved (and only temporarily). Thus, it was inevitable that without changing their pattern (which they would not do), the relationship would not last.

∼

Mark and Jane had a marriage that had continued for many years after each of them lost their sexual desire for each other. They both claimed that there was no fulfillment, but when either would make a gesture to leave the relationship, the other would pull out all the stops in order to make the marriage continue. As Mark said, "When I think I'm losing her, I want her back, and when it appears as though she's not leaving, I become distant again." Incidentally, Mark had a parallel relationship with another woman (also married), which Jane didn't know about. Jane confided to me in private that she had strayed occasionally, but with "no one special." Each was in what I refer to as a "comfortable state of discomfort," where they do not want to interrupt that status quo. When they are not in crisis, they are, at best, compatible roommates (their grown children were from previous marriages). For Mark and Jane, the passion in their relationship has died a slow death, but they are so enmeshed in other ways that no one is willing to take the first step. They ended couples' therapy still in limbo. In other words, neither was willing to leave, and neither was willing to do anything significant to change the situation. Scenarios like theirs are far from uncommon.

Some Bottom Lines to Consider

Many people think that in order to end a marriage (or other type of love relationship) you literally have to despise the individual from whom you are separating — or at the very least, consider their feelings to be unimportant. Not so! *With rare exceptions, a relationship that is not serving both of you is not benefiting either of you in the end*. It is not only possible, but quite common to still care deeply for your partner as a person, while at the same time becoming aware that the relationship between you is just not workable.

People rarely, if ever, make significant and permanent changes in themselves merely because their partners demand that those changes be made. *Promises* are often made to appease a partner, and so are *temporary* changes. When permanent changes are made, almost without exception, they are made for yourself — *not* someone else. Unless you and your partner truly desire to make the changes that you determine need to be made to save your relationship (even if you can achieve peace by learning to accept things), at the very best you will only prolong your current situation. Changes will be permanent only if your partner clearly sees that it is to his or her personal benefit and advantage to make them. And the same goes for you. If your decision is to end the relationship, remember, there still may be times when you will painfully question your decision. There may even be periods later on when you will regret it. But waiting for that mythical absolute certainty is merely a bad strategy for burning up your most precious and irreplaceable commodity — *time!* (Perhaps even a very large portion of your life.) Even in the direst situations, it can seem far easier in the short run to stay in an unworkable relationship situation, rather than face the immediate pain of separation. Thus, while for many the task is to learn *relationship skills,* for others it is to learn *how to leave.*

So, if either one of you simply no longer wants this relationship to continue, it is highly unlikely that it could continue as anything other than a perfunctory living arrangement. When do you know that a relationship has truly run its course? Any of these three signals should be taken very seriously:

• You and/or your partner do not want to stay in the relationship, and one or both of you have no desire to work on resolving the issues.

• There is no longer a desire for you to spend time together, and neither of you feels motivated to increase your tolerance of each other, work on your indifference, or be involved in each other's life.

• The magnitude of stress is so great that it causes you physical or emotional problems that can be attributed to the relationship.) And remember, often in this case the symptoms of distress disappear when you are not together.)

Of course, you can stay together for a lifetime, as long as you don't require the relationship to be more than what it is right now. Indeed, many couples do make a lifelong commitment based on:
• the children;
• religion;
• financial necessity;
• convenience;
• social or political standing;
• addiction to the relationship;
• an unwillingness to make the lifestyle changes that separation requires; or
• a devastating fear of going it alone.

Although this is not the choice preferred by most, it has certainly become the choice of many. And most people who have stayed in relationships out of fear rather than desire (whether it be the fear of being single again or any one of the many other disguises or excuses which your fear can take on — we'll discuss them in detail in chapter 4) usually end up regretting it. Only you can decide how big a part your fears and anxieties will play in how you decide to live your life.

Are you still undecided? Many times I have seen couples stay in unfulfilling situations for inordinate periods of time (like Mark and Jane, for example). My own bottom-line belief is this:

> *If you are undecided, it is in your own best interest to leave no stone unturned in trying to save your relationship, provided that your relationship has at least the potential to add an acceptable degree of happiness and quality to your life.*

You will find the following section of this chapter as well as chapters 5 and 6 to be helpful to you with this perspective.

But remember, each day you spend in an unhappy relationship is one less day spent in a life that can bring you fulfillment, passion, comfort and happiness.

If you have determined that you must get out in order to live a life that can be fulfilling to you on a long term basis, then my advice is to do whatever it takes to recognize that your relationship has indeed run its course, and for the sake of the quality of your life, accept the reality that it cannot be saved.

In chapter 4 we will discuss strategies you can use to empower yourself to go in that direction.

Additional Strategies to Work Through Your Ambivalence

If you are still in limbo about whether your relationship can or cannot work for you in the long-term, consider some of these strategies:

• *Set a definite standard to gauge whether or not your relationship should continue.* For example, make a list of what would have to happen for you to feel a sense of peace. Are you thinking long-term or short-term? Quite often, the status quo wins in the short-term, but is your decision one that you will predictably continue to regret? Someone recently described to me this phenomenon of staying, as living with a dull low-grade ache. At the same time, she regarded leaving as a severe, intense and glaring acute pain. Only you can decide if it is preferable to have the dull ache indefinitely over the severe pain that is most likely temporary in nature. In thinking long-term, think about what you can live with for a period of from five years to the rest of your life.

• *Determine whether your passion conflicts with peace.* How would you suggest someone else (other than you or your partner) whom you truly cared about resolve this delemma? Once again, there are no right or wrong answers here, only choices for you to make. All I can do is lay them out for you (or perhaps tell you what would work for me).

• *Set a time limit.* Most relationships that aren't working are characterized by a great deal of fighting, distance, or indifference. Nobody is happy, and yet there is no immediate pressure to break up or to take steps to change things. By determining that if it doesn't get better within a specified amount of time you will separate, many couples find that their relationship takes on a higher priority. Practice has shown that this simple agreement is most effective when a couple actually sets a date. Once you have agreed upon a specific amount of time, each person can make his or her own best effort to save the relationship, knowing there is the definite reality of a possible breakup on the horizon. On the other hand, there is sometimes a sense of relief once this agreement is made simply because an end is in sight. This, too, tells you a great deal about where your relationship really is.

Trial Separations

An intermission can be helpful when at least one partner determines that it would be better not to have the other around for a while. If you choose a trial separation, observe whether the absence draws you closer or pushes you further apart. At best, a trial separation has a built-in time limit — a week, a month, six months — which enables you to think through (as well as act out) your options without the finality of the relationship being over. In addition, it gives you both a vacation from whatever chronic issues are making the potential separation imminent. During a separation everyone involved usually gets a clearer picture of what has been going on. It also gives you a better perspective of your options.

By taking the edge off the tension you feel together, and giving yourselves a bit of breathing room, your choices may become clearer as to whether you would still prefer to go your separate ways once the practical issues have been resolved, or whether getting back together is a valid option. By agreement, trial separations can be extended indefinitely until one or both of you have a better vision of what you want for the long term. I have seen trial separations last for as short a period of time as a few hours and, at the other extreme, one trial separation that actually lasted twenty-three years! It is important to find a way to get past the anger that is sabotaging your relationship, and then look at the situation as rationally as possible. Getting out of each other's way for a while might very well help you to do just that.

Some additional considerations when negotiating a trial separation:

• Have you worked out the finances so that it does not become so expensive that the trial separation itself becomes a definitive issue?

• Is each of you free to date other people?

• Will you be seeing each other at all? (If so, will you be having sex with each other?)

• Will you be talking on a regular basis?

• What other ground rules do you want to set for this period of time? (For example, what do you agree to tell or not tell each other about your activities during the time you are apart? Can you agree to a "don't ask, don't tell" or no recrimination policy? Are you both clear about the rules?)

• If children are involved, how will the trial separation be explained to them? (How and under what circumstances will the partner who leaves the house see the children?)

• Who else will be told about your trial separation, and just what will they be told? (A suggestion is that as few people as possible know about your separation as long as it is still a *trial* separation)

• Have you made sure there are no potential legal quagmires in the trial separation? (A strong suggestion is that you get a legal consult to make sure you are not creating any problems that could haunt you later on should you decide to go through with a divorce. Rules vary from place to place regarding your obligations to each other.)

Expect the unexpected. A trial separation can help you to work on yourself and find the peace that has eluded you in the relationship. On the other hand, it can also help you to realize that all along you really wanted to be together. Sometimes dating others will cause one partner to want to get back together, and have the opposite effect on the other partner. That is why it is called a "trial separation." Many couples dread the idea of going in this direction, only to find it to be a tool powerful enough to shatter whatever ambivalence remains.

For an innovative approach to the trial separation, take a look at Dr. Bruce Fisher's "Healing Separation" model in the book, *Rebuilding: When Your Relationship Ends* (Fisher & Alberti, 2000).

Getting Professional Help

There are a few times when getting *professional counseling or psychotherapy* — individually, as a couple, or both — is more appropriate. Often couples' therapy begins with the question of whether a relationship can or should be saved. In this case, the needs of three entities should be considered: yourself, your partner, and the two of you together as a unit. Even if you have determined that you would really like to get out, but are staying because of those fears that the very thought of leaving conjures up, I highly recommend individual psychotherapy. The therapist will act as an impartial observer who can help you to assess the strengths and weaknesses of your relationship and of each partner, as well as each partner's potential to provide fulfillment to the other. Therapy can be a vehicle for airing the issues — in an atmosphere of safety — for healing the relationship, or for helping one or both partners to handle whatever issues they face in splitting up (if, of course, you determine that your differences cannot be worked out).

If you have opted to enter therapy or counseling and your partner is unwilling, it may be a good idea for you to make an appointment on your own to discuss the situation. Often a therapist can help you explore bringing your partner into the process. If you are or have previously been in individual therapy, your partner may object to seeing your therapist. Honor that objection, and then together find a person you both perceive as being neutral and acceptable. Your own therapist may be as impartial as can be — even if you have been in individual therapy with that professional for quite awhile. However, your partner may not believe this, and may fear being "ganged up on." This is especially true if you are a lot more therapy-wise than your partner. If this is the case, the best course of action may be to let your partner choose the therapist.

A legal consultation is another form of professional help that may be very useful to you. Sometimes clarifying the facts about what your legal status may be, and how a divorce or separation will affect your life (with respect to your financial or legal vulnerabilities), will allay the fears that could be the major forces behind procrastination when you know (or think you know) what you want to do. In addition, a legal or financial consultation also can have the effect of putting you in touch with the reality that may make staying together a more attractive option. Getting the right consult puts you under no obligation, but can do wonders for your peace of mind. But if you do consult an attorney at a point in time where you are still ambivalent, be clear that you have not yet decided to separate or divorce. Many attorneys who specialize in divorce and other family matters tend to assume you are ready to leave, unless clearly told otherwise.

The best way to find a psychotherapist or an attorney is by word of mouth, through someone who has worked with that person, or through another professional who is familiar with the therapist's work. Your comfort level with any professional you choose to work with is paramount. You are the consumer here (as much as you are for other products or services). If a word-of-mouth referral is not an option, some other reliable sources for help can be found in the appendix of this book.

Most importantly, it is worth repeating one more time that *you will probably feel much better if you do everything you possibly can when it comes to saving a relationship which you value!* Millions have been helped in therapy, both when the relationship could be saved and when it couldn't (and a partner needed help with the transition of ending it). Moreover, it is quite rare when it does harm. I cannot urge you strongly enough to give therapy a try at any point when you feel stuck, problems surface that you simply cannot seem to resolve on your own, or you need a bit of objectivity to help you navigate an impasse.

Ambivalence is a state of mind, not a point of fact. Resolving ambivalence may not be easy, but once you do it you will have the rest of your life to reap the benefits. In the next chapter, we'll explore what leaving will be like for you if that is your choice.

4

"WHAT IF I LEAVE?" — "WILL I BE SORRY?"
AND ALL THOSE OTHER QUESTIONS YOU MAY BE ASKING

~

How often I have heard sentences that begin like this, "I would leave in a heartbeat if only..." And here are some of the many ways that sentence ends:

- "... I *knew* I wouldn't end up living on the street."
- "... I *was certain* I could meet someone else at some point and not die alone."
- "... I wasn't worried about my children; and *knew* I could still have a good relationship with them."
- "... I *had no doubt* that I wouldn't end up making the same mistake yet again — with someone else."
- "... I *was sure* I could survive emotionally."
- "... I *knew* that my partner would be all right without me."
- "... I had some place to go."
- "... I was strong enough to withstand my ex-partner's revenge."
- "... I wouldn't be ostracized by my family and/or friends."
- "... I had a career of my own."
- _____

Do any of the statements above capture *your* feelings? Is there one of your own that you could add to that blank line at the bottom of the list? If so, you might want to take a piece of paper now and write it down. Then take another piece of paper and head it up "Pros and Cons for *Ending* This Relationship." Head the left side "Pros," that is, the factors in *favor* of ending it (for example, "I will no longer be abused" or "there's little between us keeping me there other than my fear of the unknown"). On the right side of the paper put the heading "Cons," or what ending your relationship has going *against* it (such as, "missing the close family ties I have with my in-laws" or "having to give up living in a really nice home.") Draw a line down the middle of your paper and list as many items as possible, in both the pro and con columns. Be sure to list anything you can think of that you may be giving up or fearing by ending your relationship at this time. Include aspects of your partner or your lifestyle, regardless of whether what you are giving up is something you do or don't want. Make the list as comprehensive as possible. When you are finished, keep it handy, to serve as a frame of reference that can be added to as new items for your list become apparent. If your list removes any doubt as to what your next move should be, then consider the strategies in this chapter and the rest of the book to be ways of reinforcing the path you have chosen to take.

Imagine It

Using your "pro and con" list as a reference or starting point, I would like you to take a few moments to thoroughly imagine and visualize — with your eyes closed — *what your life would be like if your relationship were now to end.* (Note: Some people find it helpful when doing a visualization exercise that appears in print to record the exercise in your own voice very slowly on a tape recorder, and then play it back while your eyes are closed. Or simply read it line by line (closing your eyes at the pauses). Some also find it helpful to have someone else read it to them. Whichever method you choose, you will find this to be a most effective and powerful exercise if you simply let yourself go wherever your images take you. Whether you are reading this exercise, listening to it on a tape recorder, or having someone else read it to you, please stop where I have put the word "pause" until you are ready to continue. In fact, *be sure to pause at any point that you need to during the visualization exercise.* Most importantly, *take your time* to reflect and visualize so that you can have as complete an experience as possible.)

Here is the visualization exercise:

> *Allow yourself to thoroughly imagine your relationship ending right now. Be aware of what your life would be like. Think about the people, places and things that would — or you believe would — be a part of your life if you were now to end your relationship. How would life be different for you right now?* (Pause) *See if you can imagine a worst-case scenario.* (Pause) *Be totally aware of how you are feeling at each step of this process. Next, see if you can conjure up*

a best-case scenario, and let yourself just drift with that best-case scenario for as long as it takes. (Pause) Having imagined a best- and a worst-case scenario, see if you can find the image that would most represent the reality of how your life would be right now *were you to decide to end your relationship. (Pause) Next, go forward slightly in time to take a look at what you imagine your life* would *be like. What would be some of the joys and sorrows of the very immediate future just after your breakup? (Pause) Now, take your time and imagine what things might be like for you one month from now. (Pause) How about in one year? (Pause) How about in five years? (Pause) How about in twenty years? (Pause) What would it be like for you toward the end of your life? (Pause) At each step, imagine that you are past all of the details. What do you feel most happy about? (Pause) What are your regrets? (Pause) Take plenty of time to reflect on each of these questions.*

When you are finished with this visualization, take as many notes as possible about what you visualized, and *how the vision of your life after your relationship felt for you.* You may want to observe how it changed at each step along the way. (For example, it may feel very painful or difficult right now or in a month, but exhilarating in a year — or the other way around.) Also, be aware of what you visualized you may have "done differently" when you got way down the road five, ten, or twenty years from now, or toward the end of your life, that could still be within your power to do. And once again, take as many notes as possible. Very often people who do this imagery exercise get other thoughts about these questions later on, so keep track of how your thought process continues to evolve. Many people find it quite helpful to do this imagery exercise several times, as long as new material continues to surface.

For some, the imagery exercise can conjure up some very powerful emotions. And while some emotions can be painful, others can be quite joyous. *The answers you are seeking lie underneath those emotions.* That is why it is important to take some time to reflect on your feelings, imagining that you *have made* the determination and ended the relationship. To make this exercise *most* effective, allow yourself to stay in that visualization frame of mind where you can imagine — see, hear, live and truly feel — each image that comes up, taking notes when you open your eyes on every aspect of breaking up that comes to you, as though it were a *fait accompli.* Thus, if you find that you have a difficult time conjuring up positive images, *be especially mindful of what it is that you are seeking for yourself* by ending this relationship. Is it peace of mind? Is it freedom? Stay with it until you are able to get a clear vision of your own perception of your life after this relationship has ended. Do you see yourself alone? In a new relationship? Having children? Where do you see yourself living? In what other ways do you see your life changing? If possible, be aware of where you imagine pain versus where you imagine relief. Some people find it extremely helpful to work on all of these images until the images become so familiar that they are almost second nature.

"If I Leave, Will I Be Sorry?"

If you are staying only out of fear, consider this to be one of those "tip of the iceberg" questions that lie underneath your fears, whatever they may be. The short answer: If it has gotten to the point where you are truly unhappy, you probably will not regret it *ultimately*. But in the short run, feeling regretful (ranging from constant and severe periods of regret to occasional and mild twinges) is certainly considered normal. One of the major functions of the visualization exercise is for you to have an experience of seeing beyond the short-term.

～

Liz and Bob had been married for about fifteen years. For the last five, Liz had been aware that they were *growing apart*. She wanted to go back to school and complete her Master's degree — an idea that Bob did not support (though he did not *vigorously* oppose it either.) She had lost just about all of her sexual desire for Bob and constantly fantasized about having an affair; but realizing that it was not her style, she never went through with it. Bob refused to go into couples' therapy (believing that there was no real problem that warranted it), so Liz entered treatment herself, and discovered that this lack of fulfillment was the major factor behind her low-grade depression. Liz quickly came to the conclusion that she would rather be alone than with someone who either could not or would not be supportive of her, and with whom she could grow. Her main fear was that Bob would not take her back if she were to leave and then somehow realize that she'd made the wrong choice. After all, she explained, "the relationship was not abusive; Bob was not a bad guy at all; there was no glaring or urgent reason to leave — *simply this chronic sense of unfulfillment*." So in addition, she felt quite guilty about leaving. When she finally discussed all of this with Bob, his attitude — "If you're not happy with me, there's nothing I can do about it" — allayed her guilt. What helped her through the fear was her realization that if she left and Bob refused to let her back, as painful as it may be, it would confirm that she had made the right choice. After Liz left, during the few periods of regret she did have, she was able to remember what the emotional climate for her was: "I knew that if I were to go back without resolving the reasons why I left, it would only be a matter of time until we were in the same boat and I would leave again." Her depression is now gone, she is in graduate school, and although she has been dating periodically, Liz now believes she is close to the point where she is ready to be open to finding a new long-term relationship. Most incredibly, she believes that no matter how her life turns out at this point (regardless of whether she gets her degree or becomes involved in another relationship), she is ultimately better off. In Liz's case, the key to managing her regrets was to compare her current (post-relationship) situation with what *she had* (with Bob) — as opposed to what she fantasized her marriage *could have been* if Bob had been a different person. Liz also came to realize that the alternative to leaving her marriage was to die emotionally and spiritually. She now wonders what she was thinking when she felt so ambivalent. If you're second-guessing your own decision to leave, try this: Honestly compare your life without the relationship to how it *really* was with the relationship. (Be realistic here: forget about how you wished it was, or how it might have been). I've found that such a comparison helps to clarify the issue, and confirms the decision to leave — even though things may now seem difficult at times.

~

Marcia and Fred had a marriage that had been on the rocks for quite some time. Marcia's *addiction to painkillers and alcohol* has been growing worse, and she refused to get any help. When Fred spoke of leaving, Marcia would threaten him with severe legal and financial consequences. The prospect of "losing his shirt" intimidated him and he would once again temporarily give up the idea. A simple legal consultation helped him to put his fears into perspective, and with virtually no ambivalence at all, he filed for divorce. *Fred's situation attests to the power of information.* If leaving is your choice, but you are holding back because of naiveté about whether or how you will be able to handle some aspect of your life afterwards (such as getting financial aid, housing, child care, whether you can lose your pension, or obtaining credit), spare no effort in finding out the truth. An angry partner who feels threatened or highly distressed by your leaving will often pull out all the stops in helping you to convert your concerns into nightmares! If such a situation is likely to be a factor in your case, make a list of your fears, and then turn them into questions that can be answered through your own solid research or with the help of an appropriate professional. (For example, if your fear is: "I will be taken to the cleaners," pose the question to your accountant or financial advisor: "What in reality will be my financial situation following my divorce?")

～

Al and Francine's thirty-year marriage had similar overtones. Francine knew that her mental health depended on leaving what she described as a highly abusive marriage. Her fear was that of becoming a "bag lady," of aging and, subsequently, dying alone. This, in Francine's words, kept her "addicted to the relationship." The alternative of staying — as she saw it — was "to die emotionally from her stifling, though financially comfortable marriage." Francine had to identify just what she needed to have in her life in order to survive in the world without the protection (however costly in terms of her happiness and quality of life) of her marriage to Al. Francine discovered that leaving was difficult, but not impossible. She was able to do it with some help:

- support of several of her women friends (who, when made aware of her situation and fears, made it clear that they were not surprised based on what they had observed),
- a job counselor (she was highly employable as an R.N.),
- encouragement in pursuing some of her creative outlets (which she had all but abandoned in recent years), and
- some information about affordable housing that would be available.

～

Carl made a decision to leave his *joyless marriage* with Lisa in an effort to — as he describes it — "salvage the rest of my life." His main fears concerned the impact his leaving would have on their two children, ages 9 and 6. The couple had given up even trying to resolve their many issues, as all serious discussions about the marriage resulted in nasty arguments. It can never be easy when young children are involved (or even older ones, for that matter!). But aside from what staying in a relationship like this does to the partners, the effect on the children needs to be weighed.

Are the children better off in an intact home with arguing parents and/or an icy environment? If Carl and Lisa choose to stay together, can they at least control the arguing (or put it far enough in the background) in order to protect the children? Or are the kids really better off with parents who don't live together, but who can relate to them separately in a more peaceful environment?

The answers to these questions certainly vary with a child's age, the intensity of what is happening at home, and each parent's level of maturity (which I will, in this case, define as their ability to subordinate their own issues to those of the kids) and their devotion to the kids. A thorough examination of all these issues (as well as visitation and single parenting) is well beyond the scope of this book. (In the appendix I suggest some other sources of reading that will be helpful to you.) But there are, however, some rules of thumb: Children need to have their own relationship — with as much stability with each parent as possible. This means a reliable visitation routine, two parents who continually assure children (when it comes up) that *they* are not in any way at fault for the divorce, and, most importantly, two parents who, no matter how tempting it may be at those times when they are angry, *never — ever — badmouth each other to or in front of the kids!* Carl left, realizing that when all things are considered, everyone would be better off.

It is an over-simplification to assume that children are going to be destroyed or even harmed because of your breakup. To the extent that you will not be the primary custodial parent, as long as you *maintain consistency* with your children, in that they know when they are going to see you and how to reach you practically anytime the need arises — regardless of how important *you* may think it is — most of the other issues can be worked out. Here's what some children said when I asked how the breakup of their parents has affected them:

- "I'm glad he left! I am very afraid of him."
- "I miss my Dad very much."
- "Now that they split up, they finally get along, and even when they're together it's way quieter and more peaceful."
- "I now have another place to go on weekends and when things get rough at home. Of course, I'd rather have my parents together, but it's not nearly as bad as I thought it would be."
- "It's much less tense around the house."

Experience has shown that what is ultimately better for the kids usually will ultimately best serve the parents as well. *Remember, you're not leaving your children!*

～

Vera described her marriage to George as one that had lost its *positive passion* a long time ago; the only passion left was the *negative passion* — rage — expressed by both when they fought. George had slowly begun to develop a drinking problem. As unhappy as Vera was, George actually described himself (when they were not fighting) as content with the way things were. Vera had long seen the marriage as being hopeless. The few times when she approached the subject of leaving, George threatened suicide. This would understandably stop Vera in her tracks. However, she had finally come to the point where this threat could no longer govern her life. She saw herself as being ruled by her guilt (at the thought of George taking his life) versus chronic unhappiness at home. She discussed her situation with a family doctor who referred her to a psychiatrist that was able to clarify her options, and explain what he thought was the nature of George's threats. He believed that they were designed to manipulate her into staying, but, of course, could not make her any guarantees. *Most mental health professionals agree that it is prudent to err in the direction of caution when one threatens suicide — under any circumstances.* Following his advice, she talked to two of George's siblings with whom she had been close, and with their help made the decision that staying was too emotionally costly for her. Within a month after she left, George was involved with another woman, but Vera would have still felt at peace with her decision to leave even if that were *not* the case.

～

Cheryl and Richard had a very intense courtship. After about six months, they decided to move in together in order to see whether to make the commitment a permanent one. Before she was involved with Richard, Cheryl had longed for this type of intensely passionate relationship. And in addition to the passion, they had a tremendous amount in common, giving them a great deal of comfort together as well. Shortly after they moved in together, however, Cheryl found that her sexual desire for Richard was starting to wane. The climate then changed and took on a negative life of its own. She later described the changes *in her* as attributable to being naïve about the fact that it is normal for sexual desire to fluctuate. Instead, she told herself that things would never be the same again. They agreed to separate — despite Richard's objections — and to date other people while determining the *long-term* direction of their relationship. It was not long before Richard became involved with someone else. Cheryl felt destroyed by this, admitted she made a mistake, and wanted to try to patch things up. At that point, Richard was uninterested in getting back together, and eventually married his new girlfriend. Five years later, at thirty-two, Cheryl is still carrying a torch for this relationship. She believes that leaving Richard was the worst mistake she has ever made in her life. She rightly attributed her actions to naiveté and perhaps immaturity, but she agrees that it is now time to let go of Richard and learn an important life lesson, instead of constantly putting herself down. Cheryl's case illustrates how regrets about leaving can first surface, and then stay around for a long time if there is an inability to let go of them. It also shows the difference between *hindsight* and *insight*. Hindsight is the attitude that underlies that destructive tendency to put yourself down — after the fact — for making what you later perceive to be an incorrect decision: "I should never have left Richard. I now believe I will never be happy without him" So hindsight is rarely helpful. However, some important insights might be: "Relationships are complex and involve two people. When an issue arises, it's important to *try to resolve it if you value the person* you are involved with, rather than to run away." "Hard as it may be, I know I can survive past the ending of a relationship I once valued." "Even if I make a seriously wrong decision, I need to learn how to forgive myself, let go of it (and him) and move on."

∿

Perhaps you see some similarities to your situation with one (or a combination) of these couples. As different as they are, these relationships all have one thing in common — someone decided to end them, after looking at the conflicts that brought them to the point of ending.

In the next section we will explore situations where *how* to end them is as difficult a decision as *whether* to end them.

"I've Decided to Leave, Now What?"

After careful consideration, I have included this section for those of you who have decided to leave, but are now struggling with *how* to do it. In my clinical practice, I have seen people stay in chronically unfulfilling and even abusive situations for years (and even decades) simply because they were unable to figure out a way to leave that would suit both their unique *needs* and *fears*. Here's what some people have said about the difficulty of leaving a relationship *that they have determined is unworkable*:

• "Maybe about six months of the cold shoulder and my partner will do me a favor and leave *for* me."

• "By refusing both to be sexual and to work on the issue, I think *my spouse* would get the message."

• "The only way I could pull it off would be *to die*."

• "I would need to take the kids to a shelter and get a restraining order."

• "We could never talk about anything meaningful when our relationship was at its best; I don't see how we could ever discuss my leaving. I would have to just disappear and leave a note."

• "I need him more than he needs me. Until this changes, I don't see how I can go anywhere. That's why the thought of leaving makes me so nervous."

• "It's a vicious circle. *My relationship is so bad that being in it is the very definition of depression.* In fact, I am so depressed that I don't have the strength to seriously think about leaving, even though I don't believe there is one bit of potential that it could possibly get better."

• "I could never leave; *I can only pray my partner will*. If this happened I would rejoice."

• "I swear my partner and I have been trying to *manipulate each other into leaving* for years, but it is never discussed and I don't know how to broach the subject."

• "He is walking on egg shells; and I am just waiting for my partner to do or say anything at all that *gives me the excuse*. Then I am out of there *without having to take the responsibility for ending it.*"

• "I would have to get his belongings to him by leaving them outside and then change the locks."

• "Maybe if I were having an *affair*..."

Here is how a few people answered this question: *If you could imagine a transition that was as close to optimal as possible, how would it play itself out?*

• "We would sit down, have a talk about what is inevitable, and then discuss how we can pull it off with as little pain as possible to either of us."

• "After settling what needs to be settled between the two of us, we would each talk to the kids and do our very best to *help them get through it.*"

• "We would find a therapist or mediator to act as a referee, and address each other's concerns so that we can each leave with as much dignity as possible."

Into which of these categories of responses would your situation fit?

Brenda and Peter were able to sit down and discuss the circumstances under which they would separate so well that for one fine moment they had second thoughts! "We have never, in twenty-seven years of marriage, been able to discuss a difficult issue as well as we were able to discuss leaving," Brenda observed. Peter echoed this, "Yes, what a shame that this had to be the issue we learned how to communicate on, but that's the way it is." Brenda and Peter were able to work out every detail of leaving, including who would get what, how they would tell people, and even how they would be supportive of each other in the process! Their decision to split was one that was mutual. Their only child was a freshman in college. And that (becoming empty-nesters) was the milestone they were waiting for in order to separate.

I believe that any couple who is willing to do whatever it takes to work together, and accept the reality of their situation, can follow some variation of this theme — even if it requires the help of a third party. A sleeper benefit is that cooperation can (by some estimates) make your collective legal fees a mere fraction of what they would be when there are battles over every single issue. But *peace is priceless, and worth every penny of it!*

However, when your partner is either vehemently opposed to the breakup, or harbors so much resentment that he or she will do anything within his or her power (and perhaps even some things that are *not* within that power) to sabotage a smooth transition for the inevitable ending of a relationship that cannot continue, then you could be left with no choice other than:

living under extremely acrimonious and *un*peaceful circumstances, or;

doing whatever is necessary in order to gain the strength to leave — so as to retake your life and be able to finally live a peaceful existence.

But *"Breaking Up Is Hard to Do"* (or at Least Can Be!)

Some people are in the situation of knowing that leaving is the only alternative, but find *the actual task of ending the relationship* (telling their partners and children, knowing what steps to take, and preparing themselves emotionally) to be an obstacle *so* intimidating and difficult to face, that it becomes as much of an issue as the relationship itself. Here is a sampling of what helped some to accomplish what they knew they needed to do:

• "We went back and forth for three days almost non-stop, having the discussion I dreaded and rehashing everything. Finally it was all on the table, and we both felt a whole lot better — maybe even from exhaustion. I was out of the house within a month. It was definitely the right thing to do. And I have to admit, not as bad as I thought it would be. But I feared that talk so much, that now, four years later, I realize *I could still be there if I had waited for it to be easy.*"

• "I made it a point to talk to several friends who had been through it, and with *their* help and support, came to understand what I needed to do and how to do it."

• "I practiced and rehearsed telling her about fifty times until I knew it by heart, and felt confident that I could go through with it and remain strong. Then and only then was I ready!"

• "The hardest part was telling my children. We all cried together. But I reassured them I loved them, would see them every week, and would be available to them by phone 24/7."

• "I wrote my spouse a long letter (that took me weeks to compose) saying all of the things I knew I couldn't get out verbally, and asked him to read it first. Then we talked. He was actually far better about it and towards me than I would ever have given him credit for. He agreed that neither of us was happy, and that sadly, *one of us* had to be the one to initiate the breakup."

• " I saw a lawyer, and just followed his advice."

• "I role-played my side of the conversation with a friend until I had it down pat, and could get through telling my partner without falling apart. In reality, it turned out not to be nearly as bad as I had imagined it would."

• "I finally gave up waiting until there would be no unhappiness about it, and assumed that the next month or so would be hell. *It wasn't easy, but it wasn't hell either.* I was actually proud of myself because I could take charge of my life for the first time in quite a while. Still there is some sadness from time to time. I accept that."

Some in that situation have even identified needing another relationship in order to end their current one. I first coined and described a term for this —"prebound relationship" — in my previous book, *The Art of Staying*

Together. A prebound relationship is similar to a *rebound relationship* (which is an involvement that occurs immediately, or in any case too soon *after* a breakup). The difference is simply that a prebound relationship *begins* while the prebounder is still very much involved in his or her last relationship — which is typically an unfulfilling or downright unhappy one. However, both rebound *and* prebound relationships have one thing in common: they serve as that combination of anesthesia and/or a safety net to aid the prebounder in breaking away emotionally. Cara describes it this way:

> "My marriage to Vernon had been dead for a long time. I guess you can say it was a classic case of terminal burnout. Joe and I met — of all places — in the supermarket. I had never strayed before, but there was such chemistry, that the next thing I knew we were involved in a tryst. It got very intense very quickly. I knew at that point that I had to leave my marriage. Joe provided me the strength to leave — something I would never have done on my own. We only stayed together for about a month or two after I left and got my own place. Then just as suddenly as it heated up, it cooled down (it turns out we really had nothing other than that animal magnetism in common). I thought it was the real thing, and was quite sad when I discovered that it wasn't. But then I realized that at least it served the purpose of getting me off the dime and out of my marriage."

Cara's story is one that is far more common than I had thought! The other typical variation of a prebound relationship happens more deliberately. Russ, whose marriage had also been characterized by indifference, began attending "singles only" events and doing other activities to (quite consciously) meet another woman. He met Charlotte at a singles bar, and began to see her regularly — never hiding the fact that he was in a marriage that was about to end (of course he wasn't as clear with her about the fact that meeting someone in her role was essential to his ending it). With Charlotte on his side, he had the impetus to leave — something he had procrastinated doing for years.

Some other variations on this theme include:

• *Having an affair, getting caught (consciously or unconsciously), and then leaving on the momentum of your partner's rage at you.*

• *Having one affair (tryst, parallel relationship or emotional affair) after another.* As long as these involvements are *undetected,* they act as the "sugar that helps the medicine go down." Once one is detected, it can serve as a prebound relationship. Some people have actually gotten *their partner* to have an affair by suggesting it — or even arranging it!

• Increasing addictive behavior (e.g., drugs, alcohol, eating disorders, gambling, internet sex/chat room activities, or spending money) can serve the purposes of self-medicating, as well as isolating yourself from your partner and possibly incurring his or her wrath, which eventually results in a breakup that you did not have to initiate!

Am I advocating any of these "creative termination procedures"? No. I — and most professionals — would much rather guide you toward a more straightforward approach when one needs to be taken. I am merely reporting to you how common they are. In fact, they are done so commonly that I felt I would be remiss by not including them. Do I then condemn them? Again, no! For many, they served at the time as their only solution or way out of a bad situation. As I have and will consistently say throughout this book, *nobody can ultimately make your choices except you*. And certainly, nobody (and I really mean *nobody*, quite literally) who hasn't walked in your shoes has earned the right to judge you. And that eliminates just about every potential judge!

Some Additional Considerations for Leaving
Here are some additional points you may wish to factor in:

• If you are still telling yourself "I failed," or "My relationship failed," make every effort to reframe that belief to the alternative, "My relationship has run its course." If you work hard at allowing this affirmation to take hold in your belief system, you will be amazed at how your negative feelings — such as anger and guilt — will change.

• As hard as it may be, force yourself to see whatever decision(s) you are making in *a positive light*. For example, if you are telling yourself, "It's terrible that I spent all these years in that lousy relationship," reframe that to, "I now have the rest of my life and every opportunity ahead to find the fulfillment that has eluded me."

• Remember that quite possibly you may experience bouts of regret, no matter what decision you make. When this occurs, always refer back to the *reasons for making your decision*. (That's another reason it's so important that you write them down!) If you do this, you will find that gradually those bouts will become fewer and fewer until they are truly a rare occurrence.

• When second-guessing yourself, always refer to your relationship *as it was when you made the decision* — not as it was in the beginning, at its best, or as you fantasized it could be.

• Allow yourself to acknowledge that no matter how bad it was when you split, there were still some good times. *Remember, relationships are way too complex to be thought of in black-and-white terms.* The realities and truth of any situation are always your best and most lasting frame of reference.

• If you decide to *reconcile,* do so *only after you have resolved the issues that were responsible for the breakup;* at the very least, use the "honeymoon period" to develop a firm strategy to vigorously work on them. This includes *genuinely forgiving each other* and letting go of anything and everything either of you may be angry about. Otherwise, it is most likely that they will resurface once again with a vengeance—and another breakup. There are no guarantees that your new life apart will be without major obstacles to overcome (see chapter 7). And indeed, things may not work out right away as you had expected. But going back as a way of soothing your short-term pain (or merely out of your addiction to your partner, the relationship, or a coupled lifestyle) is rarely the ultimate answer either. Unless there is a real — not imagined — reason to believe that *things will be different this time* (such as a long-term resolution of the issues that caused the breakup), going back could amount to little more than another variation of a rebound relationship.

• It bears repeating; *you are not leaving your kids!*

• If you are worried about what others think of you in the context of splitting up, remember this simple truism — *what others think of you is none of your business!*

• *Take some time to reflect on the relationship that has just ended,* and make a long list of things that you have learned, about yourself and about relationships, that you would not want to repeat when next you become involved. These insights are now fresh, but are often easily forgotten. They are invaluable to you, because you learned them the hard way! Wisdom right now can be defined as your ability to *learn from all that has taken place.* For example, if your last relationship started as a whirlwind romance, make sure that your next partner is someone who actually *likes and supports you,* in addition to all the passion you may initially share!

• If your relationship has ended, be aware of what *your* bottom line was in ending it. See if you can condense it into a sentence or two, put it on a 3x5 card and carry it in your wallet for reference whenever you need to refer to it, such as when you find yourself second guessing. Examples of this bottom-line statement could be:

— "I could no longer be in a relationship that was governed by fear rather than desire."

— "I decided no longer to stay in a marriage only because I felt too guilty to leave."

— "Genuine inner peace is not possible with _____ (name of your ex-partner)."

— "I will never again stay with someone who doesn't love or care about me."

— "I need to cut my losses… we don't get wasted time back!"

In the next chapter we will give this same treatment to the option of *staying together*.

5

"What If I Stay? Could I Be Missing A Better Life?"

~

I t is not at all unusual to be exploring the questions in this chapter with as much intensity — or even more — as you experienced while struggling with the issues of chapter 4. The previous chapter had you look at the prospect of *leaving*. In this chapter, we will explore the case for *staying*. Then we'll have looked at all of the pieces in that ambivalence puzzle.

So before going any further, please take out another clean sheet of paper, and again draw a line down the middle, putting "Pros" on the left side and "Cons" on the right side of the line. Now head this up, "Pros and Cons for *Staying* in this Relationship." Again, just as you did in chapter 4, list as many items as you can think of for *both* the "pro" (for example, *"I won't have to turn my life upside down financially"* or *"It would be so much better for the kids"*) and "con" (such as, *"I would have the opportunity to meet the person I've always wanted my partner to be"* or *" the anger we can't resolve is bringing me down in every area of my life"*) sides of your paper. Keep this list, and be sure to add to it — at any time — as more things occur to you. Take notice of whether there are any items on your list — pro or con — that are *so powerful* that they make any of the other issues seem almost irrelevant. (If this is the case, perhaps the decision-making process is over, and now your task is to implement your decision. But even then, read on.)

Next, we will do a similar visualization exercise to the one in chapter 4. Only this time I would like you to *imagine staying in your present relationship,* using your list of "pros" and "cons" as a starting point. Take this opportunity to really get into a frame of mind of what it would be like for you if your relationship were to continue into the future (perhaps looking five years down the road). Once again, the visualization exercise that follows can either be read by you (closing your eyes at the pauses to do the visualization), recorded on a tape recorder and listening with eyes closed throughout the entire exercise (simply stopping the tape as you need time to pause and visualize), or read by someone else to you at the pace you've chosen. I have included the suggested places for you to pause throughout this visualization exercise.

So close your eyes and:

> *Imagine what staying in your relationship would feel like. Think about the people, places, and things that would be or continue to be a part of your life if you were to stay. As you go along, picture details of scenes in your life. Take all the time you need to feel and experience any emotions that come up for you.* (Pause and stay with each aspect of this exercise for as long as you would like in order to be able to see all the visions emerge, feel all of the emotions that come up, and allow yourself to process any insights that may arise.) *Become aware of what it is you would now need to do in order to keep your present relationship intact.* (Pause) *Next, see if you can conjure up a* best-case *scenario, and just let yourself just drift with that best-case scenario of staying together for as long as it takes.* (Pause) *Then do the same for what you imagine to be your* worst-case *scenario.* (Pause) *Having imagined both a best- and a worst-case scenario of what your life would be like by staying together, see if you can find the image that most represents the* reality of how your life would be right now *were you to decide to stay. And imagine what you would feel regarding your decision toward yourself, your partner, and all those relevant people who are important to you. Be especially aware of any joys or sorrows that come up.* (Pause) *Let yourself slowly drift from* right now *to next month. What would your life be like in a month if the decision you made were to stay, and you were able to put any thoughts of leaving behind you?* (Pause) *A year from now?* (Pause) *In five years?* (Pause) *Twenty years?* (Pause) *Take all of the time you need to return to and experience any phase of your visualization that you feel drawn to. Then slowly, let your vision extend toward the end of your life.* (Pause) *When you are good and ready, and you have seen all there is to see* for right now, *slowly open your eyes.*

Next, take as many notes as you possibly can about what you visualized, and how the vision of your life *with your relationship continuing* felt for you. Observe how the vision of your partner and lifestyle may have changed at each step along the way. (For example, you may feel relieved in the short run, but might find yourself regretful about it as more time goes by — and especially towards "the end of your life"; or the other way around — more difficulty now, but much better off in the long run.) Also, be aware of how *what you visualized became different* as you got down the road five, ten, or twenty years from now, or toward the end of your life (observing what you may have wished then you could do now). If you allow yourself to take them in, those *specific visions* could be great gifts, since you obviously still have all the options that exist at this point of time open to you. So take as many notes as possible to ensure that this information is not lost, when in fact it can always be available to you as an important reference. Expect that you might get other thoughts about these questions later on. If so, be aware of them; and keep track of how your thought process continues to evolve. You may find it very helpful to practice this imagery exercise several times, as long as new material continues to surface.

By doing this visualization exercise along with the one in chapter 4, you have taken the opportunity to preview in detail *both possible directions* that your decision to stay or leave would take you. If you were *only* able to concentrate on a best- (or worst-) case scenario, try the visualization (or both of the visualizations) again. Only this time, *force yourself* to focus on what a worst-case scenario would be like (or vice versa). You may even find it helpful to do it an additional time *without* necessarily seeking a best or worst case scenario. The real mission for this visualization tool is to permit yourself to take this opportunity to look ahead — with as much intensity as you will allow yourself — at every possible option.

When you are finished, take careful notice of how every one of your options feels to you. What were each of them like? And, most importantly, don't forget to go ahead and repeat each visualization as often as you need to until you get all of the clarity you are seeking! Doing this is likely to open up a whole new dimension for you. A visualization exercise such as this (which relies only on *your inner resources*) can be the best and most reliable source of information you can find anywhere to resolve whatever ambivalence is left.

"If I Stay, Could I Be Missing a Better Life?"
Here are what some said they would miss by staying in their present relationships:

- "I've always had the *fantasy* of meeting the ideal person for me — a soul mate or dream partner. I know I certainly don't have that now, and don't know if I can *or want* to give that fantasy up by closing the door to finding it."
- "The *peace and quiet* of living alone."
- "The *fun single life* I never had (because I married so young), and all the freedom that goes along with it."
- "The kind of *intense passion* that I experienced when I was having an affair that I haven't been able to feel in my marriage for a long time (if ever)."
- "The *opportunity to travel* and see the world — something that is for the most part incompatible with this relationship."
- *"Financial freedom."*
- "More *time to devote to my career* without time and energy conflicts."
- "A chance to see if I can really be happy with myself and my life without having to view everything through the specter of this marriage."
- "The *opportunity to grow* and explore new things in ways that this relationship stifles me."
- *"I wish I knew, but there's no way I could possibly know right now, so why ask?"*

That last response comes about as close to what *my* short answer would be to the question ("If I Stay, Could I Be Missing A Better Life?"). *So why ask the question?* Because it is a question that forces us to explore — not so much the answer, *but why you might have asked it in the first place.*

Now, let's explore the question that *can* be answered. The one that will make that other *un*answerable one unnecessary:

What does your partner need to do in order for you to let go of that last trace of ambivalence? (Remembering, of course, that this taken literally could be an awfully high standard, since it is perfectly normal to have some small twinges of ambivalence — at least until the decision to re-commit is made, and perhaps even beyond that.)

Here are a few answers from others who are struggling with the question of how they'd like their partners to change:

- "Give up his/her affair (or resolve the sexual addiction)."
- "Move to a certain area (other than where we are living)."
- "Give up his/her career (or career change) or a certain aspect of it."

- "Spend more time at home and less time working and shutting me out."
- "Stop smoking."
- "Be neater/cleaner."
- "Lose fifty pounds."
- "Have a child."
- "Have an abortion."
- "Be more responsive to me sexually" (often in a very specific way).
- "Be less sexually demanding of me/respect my sexual limits."
- "Support me in my career change."
- "Earn a decent living."
- "Give up certain friends."
- "Be more sociable with (or accepting of) certain people who are important to me."
- "Stop drinking (drugging, gambling, overeating or over-spending)."
- "Spend less time on the computer (or in chat rooms, etc.)."
- "Let mother (father, sister, brother, children, etc.) live with us."
- "Have mother (father, sister, brother, children, etc.) move out."
- "Stop blaming me for everything that goes wrong."
- "Show a willingness to sometimes give in to my point of view."
- "Show me I am needed."
- "Be able to argue without being vicious and abusive."
- "Become a better parent (more or less protective/more involved/less enmeshed)."
- "Go with me to counseling, now."

How would you answer the question: *What does your partner need to do in order for you to resolve your ambivalence in favor of staying?* Make a list of the things that *your partner would need to do in order for you to recommit at this point.* The key word is "do" (as opposed to "be"). The word "do" implies that there is a change in behavior *within your partner's capability* that could vastly improve the climate. For example, if your criterion for staying is for your partner to *be more attractive,* you are making an unreasonable and perhaps impossible demand. But if what you are requesting is that he or she *lose fifty pounds, bathe more often,* or *have better table manners,* you have at least put out a request that is possible to fulfill and/or can be negotiated.

Next, consider whether and how your requests (or demands) can be negotiated. Give each item on your list a value — from one to ten — according to how negotiable your request may be. A "1" is something that is completely negotiable, while a "10" would be totally *non-negotiable*. In other words, a deal breaker, or certain end to the relationship if that demand — and "demand" is certainly the proper word when you are talking a "10" — is not met. For example, if your partner's temper has the potential of delivering a fatal blow to your relationship, asking that he or she be less angry (as we previously discussed) is way too vague. But agreeing to *refrain from loud arguing* — that is ending any discussion until an issue can be addressed without the furious overtones that you may consider abusive to you — is a *valid request. Participating in couples' therapy* to help him or her do this could be another valid request. It's valid, in that it is clear, doable and negotiable. Most importantly, rate each of these items on that "negotiability scale" from one to ten. Some couples in your situation have only one or two items on their list, while I have seen others with lists of literally dozens of items. *Your mutual willingness to do what it takes to support each other through the changes you both find important could be the magic ingredient that takes your relationship off of life support!*

Also, be aware of the various sub-issues. For example, if an important issue for you is relocating because of your partner's job, be sure to take all of the *sub-issues* such as each of the logistics of your move into consideration. By breaking a major task or problem down to manageable pieces, that overwhelming feeling might disappear.

Working It Out Together

When you are clear on the tangible specific changes that your partner can make, consider how your negotiation process will take place. Here are some guidelines for that process:

• *Never negotiate when angry!* Think about it. Have you ever *truly* resolved anything in the heat of a battle? Good negotiation requires cool heads. If there are issues that are so sensitive that make this impossible, consider getting some help from a third-party rather than letting it permanently drag you down. *Avoid ultimatums* or any other statements that will predictably prompt your partner to react defensively or declaring, "all bets are off."

• *Show your willingness to listen to his or her point of view as well.* Your partner may actually have a point! And whether or not you ultimately agree with it, *at least know what that point of view is.* Giving in occasionally never killed anybody, but it has saved many relationships.

• *Some of your issues have been around for a long time, and have been argued about endlessly — but never talked about.* Chances are that if you keep an open mind, you will learn something that you have not known before. This may give you a different perspective on the issue (or it may not). But don't cheat yourself of the opportunity to find out.

• *Discuss one — and only one — issue at a time.* And don't let things get out of hand! If you lose your focus, one of you should blow the whistle to stop the discussion until you can get back on track.

• *Be as clear as possible when sharing your expectations of each other.* You are looking for *long-term solutions* to what may have been long-standing problems. Allow that your expectations may never be met one hundred percent (remember, does perfection even exist?), but at the same time, you don't want to be at this same impasse a month or a year from now.

• *Settle for nothing less than a win-win solution!* Think in terms of "what's good for you needs to be good for me" (and vise versa). Almost without exception, anything else will come back and bite you at a later date. Many people will agree to anything when they are negotiating out of desperation to keep their relationship from ending. But experience has shown that once the immediate crisis is over, a partner who is not *truly on board* with the resolution of the issue in question will invariably revert back to the way things were.

(Note: For an expansion of many of the above strategies, as well as numerous additional ones geared toward issue resolution with your partner, please see chapter 6.)

How Have Other Couples Worked It Out?

David and Joan were on the verge of splitting. Joan complained that although she loved David, she was not "in love with him." She saw her decrease in sexual desire as a sign that their marriage had ceased to be fulfilling enough for her to continue in it. Yet, David was someone she still loved and admired very much as a person, and she was unwilling to call it quits as long as there was any possibility that they could save their marriage. In my experience, the loss of sexual desire (when there is not a physical reason) is usually a symptom of underlying anger about one or more unresolved issues. With David and Joan, it went back to about two years earlier. Joan wanted to have a baby while she still could; she was approaching her fortieth birthday. David was vehemently opposed, and Joan acquiesced — giving up the idea. Shortly thereafter, she began to gradually lose her sexual desire for David until it was just about gone. By identifying this underlying issue, David found that he was unaware of Joan's intense desire to be a parent. He loved Joan, and did not want to lose her. After much consideration, he actually suggested that if it were too late for her to conceive, he would be willing to adopt a child (if that was what she really wanted). David's offer (without at all being prompted or given an ultimatum) truly assured Joan that he cared about something that was extremely important to her. With that, her sexual desire started to return — and has been getting stronger and stronger — as a result of resolving her anger regarding their disagreement over this issue and how David initially dismissed it.

~

Alicia and Jay both have strong personalities and vastly different parenting styles. Jay was quite strict, while Alicia was just as permissive. They had many bitter arguments about the problems caused by these differing views. At one point, Jay thought that a separation would be the best thing for everyone. This way they could each have their own relationship with the kids, and would not be triggered by what they saw as each other's "opposite" behavior. They made an agreement among themselves that they would separate after the Christmas holidays. As soon as they agreed to this, they started to have the type of warm feelings toward each other they had not experienced in quite a while (actually since the discipline of the kids had become an issue). Moreover, Jay realized that he did *not* want to live separate from the kids either. With this impending separation as a wake-up call, they agreed to work very hard at negotiating a middle ground for how they would discipline the children. They agreed they would also support each other, and that whenever they came up against obstacles that made this hard to do, they would take at least a one-hour intermission before discussing ways to find that cherished common ground. Children often provide both *good reasons* for working things out (such as in the case of Alicia and Jay) as well *excuses* for staying together. (How often I have heard some variation of, "I would leave this second were it not for the kids!")

~

Jake and Terri have been married for almost twenty-five years. Jake has had several affairs that pretty much amounted to trysts with women who knew his marital status, and that he was not available for anything more than merely a sexual liaison. Terri is a minister's daughter, described by friends and family (Jake included) as "a great wife and mother." In addition, they have much in common and genuinely like and care about each other, but their sex life has been (in Jake's words) very "ultra-traditional." For Jake, this was a euphemism for *dull* — thus, the affairs. When Terri caught Jake in a lie about where he had been, and he admitted to her that he was with another woman, Terri was crushed and, as an initial reaction, thought that there was no alternative but divorce. After the dust settled and she was able to understand Jake's frustration with their sex life (he never did admit to her that there had been *several* of these affairs over the years), she was able to see what *her role* was in Jake's behavior. She agreed to try some new sexual variations, and he agreed to stay monogamous. Stay tuned.

Changing Your Expectations

Beware of what I call the "Soul Mate Syndrome," which is the highly unlikely idea that the partner you should be with will effortlessly be a perfect match for you in every way. Logic dictates that *the higher your expectations are of each other, the more difficulty you will have in meeting those expectations!* Your expectations are highly personal matters; nobody else really can say (better than you, of course) what yours should be. But sometimes simply realizing how your expectations of your partner — and/or of relationships in general — have sabotaged you can make the difference between wanting to stay and wanting to go:

• Christine: "I realized that if you had a relationship with someone who agrees with you one hundred percent, then what's the sense of there being *two* of you?"

Insight: *Total agreement is an unattainable fantasy.*

• Bill: "Can you believe I wanted someone with absolutely *no quirks*? No wonder I had problems with every relationship I was in."

Insight: *People without "quirks" do not exist.*

• Jennifer: "What helped me was to realize that if I adopted the attitude with a man that 'what you see is what you get,' I could stop putting all this energy into trying to change him (which invariably burns me out and turns him off)."

Insight: *Letting your partner be who he is makes things so much easier.*

• Matt: "I've finally given up the fantasy of having the perfect relationship. Now I have one that's merely *perfect enough.*"

Insight: *Perfect relationships don't exist, either.*

• Joyce: "When I think of staying with Jim for the rest of my life, I feel a weird sensation of being trapped. After all, the rest of my life is hopefully a long, long time. But *when I think of staying with him for now or the foreseeable future, I no longer have the desire to leave.* I know that I can always entertain the prospect of leaving, if I need to."

Insight: *Forever exists only in theory. Life is best lived a day (week, month) or — perhaps when applying the principle to deciding whether your relationship can stay together — a year at a time.*

• Patrick: "I used to think that I stayed because I didn't want to interrupt the status quo in my life or the lives of my wife and children. So I always had one eye out the window. I now realize I'm here because I want to be. That may not sound like a big thing, but just being able to say that turned my whole life around. *I no longer tell myself that the 'grass is greener on the other side of the fence.'*"

Insight: *Beware of those vague fantasies of nirvana to which you may be comparing the real life you have."*

• Jim: "It took the prospect of losing a relationship I really valued to realize that *good relationships require work.* They can't operate on automatic pilot. I guess I always had the idea that efforts in improving communication or sex weren't necessary in good relationships."

Insight: *Perhaps the biggest myth of all is that the best relationships are automatically good. With rare exceptions, how good or excellent your relationship will be depends on how much effort you expend to make it that way.*

• Lori: "I discovered not only how to stay together, but how to feel a whole lot more peaceful in the process by simply letting him be who he is without trying to make him something else. After all, he's the man I fell in love with. *And even better, when I do that, he reciprocates!*"

Insight: *You can choose peace by giving your partner the acceptance he or she deserves, or turmoil by withholding it.*

All of these couples are still together. They (and I) consider the wisdom contained in these insights to be an important reason they were able to save their relationships. Perhaps this is a good time to see if a similar statement can serve as a resolution for you.

Here's to the End of Your Ambivalence

Here are some additional considerations and strategies to help you resolve your ambivalence in the direction of staying:

• Whenever your relationship ambivalence rears its ugly head, *go back to your best and worst visions* of what life would be like if you were to stay or leave. In reconciling those best and worst visions, you can get an incredibly sharp view of the *big picture.*

• *Keep your eye on the ball.* And with respect to relationships, that means trying to work out ways to change your and your partner's *behavior — not your personalities.* The more precise you can be regarding just *what the behavior is that needs to change*, the greater is your chance for success. Trying to make your partner (or anyone else for that matter) something he or she is not is an exercise in futility that is destined to fail!

• How realistic is the fantasy of having everything you could possibly want in one partner? Not very! (Do you know of any *real* examples — of people you know personally — where this is the case?) But the worst of all worlds, if you decide to stay, is to harbor that fantasy. So if you stay, make every effort to let go of any expectations of perfection you may have, then make a commitment to work through your issues — *by changing what can be changed while accepting everything else* — as best you can.

• *Never compare an outside affair with your primary relationship.* Comparing the passion of an extramarital liaison with your marriage (or primary relationship) is like comparing apples and oranges, or fantasy with reality. Few primary relationships can come out ahead with that kind of comparison. Unless you have been caught, your partner asks specifically, or it is absolutely necessary for some other reason, be very cautious about whether it is in the best interest of everyone concerned to confess an affair. *For many people that is a relationship breaker, regardless of what else is going on.* If you have discovered that your partner has had an affair, avoid the immediate temptation to write your partner off forever. Take my word for one thing: Although many relationships do (and perhaps should) split up because of extramarital activities, many others have been made a lot stronger because of their ability to survive them.

• The lack of sexual desire can have many causes, including anger, depression, anxiety, the side effects of certain medications, numerous medical conditions, as well as some normal developmental issues (such as aging or menopause). The Appendix contains additional reading materials that addresses this topic. If you or your partner are experiencing any sexual difficulty, I urge you to have it properly evaluated by a qualified medical and/or mental health professional. Treatment for inhibited sexual desire, as well as other sexual dysfunctions, is readily available and has an extremely high rate of success. *No relationship that you value is worth throwing away without a thorough evaluation of these types of conditions.* Additionally, as each partner ages, sex may become a bit *less* effortless than it was before; a partner may require more foreplay or stimulation, and/or some new variations to your lovemaking activities may be in order. This, too, is a natural condition that you and your partner can address as a team. Sometimes a combination of learning new sexual techniques, different attitudes, and properly prescribed medications that treat different aspects of the problem (such as depression or erectile dysfunction) can obliterate this problem.

If you have decided to recommit, consider my definition of what the true nature of a committed relationship is: *It is an agreement that you will stay together until one of you changes your mind!* That definition may sound rather tentative, but it has helped many to be able to take it *one day at a time.*

In this chapter you have explored the process of resolving your ambivalence in favor of *staying* in your relationship. In the next chapter, we will explore your new life together, along with ways to *minimize the possibility that you will change your mind.*

PART III

THE AFTERMATH OF AMBIVALENCE

~

Okay, you've worked through your confusion — or most of it. Now you're ready to use your newfound clarity to prevent yourself from slipping back into those murky waters of ambivalence.

The next two chapters assume you've moved past that ambivalence and are ready to get on with your life. Chapter 6 assumes you have decided to *stay together,* and provides you with numerous strategies for making and keeping the relationship solid, now that you have managed to save it. Chapter 7 assumes that *your relationship will end* and offers strategies for you to make the transition to your new life and lifestyle.

I consider the various chapters in this book to be "self-contained seminars," and I encourage you to think of Part III — all of it — as a seminar that will help you *clarify your choice even further.* Thus, if you have decided to *stay,* be sure to still read chapter 7, which deals with single life, and the challenges of what life would be *after* ending your relationship. If you have decided to *leave,* don't skip chapter 6, which deals with your life assuming you are to stay together.

On the other hand, perhaps your choice is not yet clear. That's often the nature of the beast. Here's a strategy that should help:

- Start by going back over Part II and doing more work with the strategies that most apply.
- Then read chapter 6 in the frame of mind that *you have decided to stay* in the relationship you are attempting to save.
- Follow that up by reading chapter 7 with the mindset of *having decided to leave.*

This approach may well become the clarifier you need.

No matter how committed to your direction you may be, these chapters in Part III will provide you with powerful opportunities for additional insight.

6
YES, IT CAN BE SAVED!
MAKING YOUR LIFE TOGETHER
REALLY WORK THIS TIME

~

You looked the prospect of a breakup, separation or divorce squarely and forcefully in the eye, and didn't like what you saw. So let's assume you have decided to stay. *Are you out of the woods?* Short answer: *If you and your partner can change whatever it was that brought your relationship to the brink of demise,* perhaps. But if you *don't* resolve the issues that came close to dooming you as a couple, probably not. In this chapter, we will explore numerous strategies designed to *keep you together* in a relationship that will serve you both.

What Could Make It Work for You this Time?
Listen to the comments of some who have either reconciled, or merely done an about-face when very close to a permanent breakup:

"I finally learned what forgiving my partner *meant — to really let go* of the things that I was angry about to the point where *I don't even think about them anymore!*"

"I realized that I couldn't just take back the traits I liked without those things I wish were different; *I now realize that I have to accept him for who he is!*"

"I now make every effort to *treat her, as I want to be treated.* This is critical."

"It's not yet what I want it to be, but *being single isn't either. And now at least we both agree that we have lots more work to do.*"

"*I now appreciate what I have in my partner.* This was not the case until I looked at the prospect of our breaking up."

"We have finally *learned to tolerate each other*; and not be so critical, particularly in the area of each other's faults."

"I simply realized that it's time to stop complaining, and to *acknowledge that my marriage is what it is.* And I am not leaving. End of story "

"I didn't really learn how to be nurturing and comforting to my partner until now."

"We finally *learned how to fight fairly* when we have to fight at all."

"When we have a disagreement or conflict, we now talk about how important the issue really is. *We try to resolve it in favor of whoever considers it most important.* Nothing has come up yet that is even close to being as important as we used to make almost everything we disagreed about."

"We no longer consider anything resolved unless we can find a *win-win* solution."

These types of revelations rarely (if ever) come about *permanently* with an apology, a hug, or a romantic interlude. Don't fall for the mythical and romanticized notions of reconciliation that you see in the movies. (Ah, but wouldn't it be nice if it did happen that way!) *When we romanticize, we infer that a relationship can effortlessly operate on automatic pilot without working on the issues that will inevitably come up.* Nothing could be further from the truth. No matter how good your relationship is, without putting some degree of effort into ensuring that it continues to be satisfactory to *both of you*, it will most likely go downhill once again. The rest of this chapter is devoted to helping you to prevent that from happening.

Creating a New Vision

If it's possible, I strongly recommend that you and your partner work on the strategies that follow *together*. However, if in your situation this is not an option, you will see there is still much that can be done with the material in this chapter (as with the strategies and tools throughout this entire book), even if your only option is to work on them alone.

It is very rare that a relationship will operate successfully in accordance with *someone else's rules*. The best relationships are custom jobs. (For example, some couples need to work on ways to spend more time together, while for others spending less together time will optimize their relationship. For some couples, taking a nice vacation together will do wonders, while for others taking *separate* vacations can be a relationship saver.) They take the unique traits, needs, concerns and idiosyncrasies of each partner into consideration. With that in mind, try this exercise — alone *or* together.

▪ *Develop a vision* (perhaps a shared one) *of what you would imagine your ideal relationship to each other would be like.* Be as specific as possible in your vision of what you want. In other words, if things were to work superbly for both of you — if you were able to permanently get past all of your difficult issues and problems; and were then able to take things to the level that you might first have imagined they could be when you originally got together:

What would be present that now is missing?

And what would be gone, that now stresses you as a couple?

Make your lists as long or as short as they need to be. But try to be as thorough as possible.

Next, compare your own relationship, as it *now exists* to the one that you have visualized. Identify every specific thing you can that separates where you now are, from what you have envisioned as ideal. Once again, this can be an individual vision, a shared vision, or both. *Is there an ideal vision that both of you can live with?* If you have identified anything that makes this vision impossible, note what that is. We will have some additional strategies later on for those things. Note what you have identified as areas where your relationship is working well, where it needs to be different, and what changes *must occur* for those problem areas to be completely addressed. *This is an exercise that can be done anytime you wish to focus on the big picture.*

Setting Relationship Goals

Here is another variation of this theme. *Write a "job description" for the role of ideal partner.* (Remember: A job description focuses on what your partner *does* for you — *never on who your partner is.* Thus, each thing in your description is something that is realistic and possible given who your partner is.) After both of you have done this — made them as thorough and detailed as necessary — exchange your descriptions and then talk about them. Most couples surprisingly find that there is little, if anything, that is not doable or negotiable in each other's ideal job descriptions.

▪ *Develop some specific goals* for what you would like to see your relationship become with respect to *specific periods of time.* Just as in business, any important project, your finances or your career — relationships need goals. Where would you like to see yourselves a month from now? Six months from now? In a year? Five years? Ten years? Ultimately? As you talk and/or think this through, *pay special attention to anything that comes up which may be standing in the way of the goals you've identified for your relationship.*

Some questions to discuss to help you clarify your goals include:

Where are we going? (With respect to our goals together, our communication, our sex life, our finances, parenting our kids, our careers, our lifestyle, etc., etc.)

Where would we like to be? (In all the important areas of life together and separately)

What obstacles are there that separate where we are now from where we want to be? (Be as specific as possible)

■ Here's another important understanding to work on: *How can you come together now in situations that would have caused you conflict and tension in the past?*

What could each of you do at such times that would be of a helpful and healing nature?

What could each of you do for the other to show support at those times?

When you see that inevitable anger cycle starting, how can one or both of you stop it in its tracks?

If you are like most couples, very rarely will you get as angry at each other the exact same way and at the exact same time. In reality, one of you probably starts getting angry first. Left unchecked, this will become contagious until the anger takes on a life of its own, and then overwhelms the issue. An excellent strategy to stop this from escalating is to *develop a code word* (like "time out", but feel free to be creative). Some couples even make their code word a humorous one, such as, "iceberg ahead!" "balloon," or "off road-rage" which means, "This is getting out of hand." For some couples, "I love you" or even a very private pet name or sexual reference does it. It is essential that you each agree to abide by that code word (and, of course, make sure that the code word never has the potential to inflame you more)! *Make it a sacred part of your relationship.* (But even if it turns out that if every once and awhile you fall off the wagon and fail to abide by it, don't negate or discard this important and possible relationship-saving strategy.) Many couples have found that the simple act of stopping their anger cycle in its tracks has meant the difference between making it (because they were then able to resolve their conflicts together) and allowing their conflicts to remain unresolved and become overwhelming and ultimately fatal to the relationship!

■ *Remember not to expect perfection from yourselves or each other.* Even when you make an "ironclad" agreement to do something a certain way and one of you slips, consider it a temporary setback, then use the strategies to get past it.

■ *When you spend time talking to each other in a meaningful way, don't focus only on problems and issues!*
- Plan *fun* things together.
- Go out on dates together — just the two of you.
- Find more ways to play at home.
- Talk about the lighter side of life.
- Give each other massages and take baths together.
- Think back to those glorious days when you were dating, when life was much simpler, and when you truly looked forward to being together permanently and sharing the things that were important to you.
- Work together to restore as much of that climate as possible — *and don't give up until you succeed!*

So talk it over, then begin to take action to *bring your relationship back to where it will be once again driven by your desire for each other,* to where you can remember the past you shared without getting caught up in the bad times, and to where you are truly together (emotionally as well as physically) because your first choice is to be together.

Learning How to Support Each Other
What kind of support do you prefer when you are feeling needy or in crisis? Knowing what your partner expects from you is crucial; not only to knowing who he or she is, but also to the ongoing climate you will share. For each person, support has a different meaning.

Unfortunately, too often people give the type of support that helps them — *the supporter* — rather than making the effort to learn what kind of support their partners — *the supportees* — respond to best. When you give your partner the kind of support that you yourself prefer, even when you do it with the best of intentions, you may find that it either doesn't work, or worse yet — it runs blatantly counter to what your partner *really wants or needs.* And when that happens, it is never without a price! Your partner may typically end up feeling negated, while you feel confused, unappreciated and perhaps angry. In this situation — nobody wins.

Some people prefer to be left alone during times of stress. If this is your preference, you may believe that leaving *your partner* alone is the best way to be supportive of him or her. But what if your partner instead prefers to have someone close to talk things over with at those times? What if your partner wants you to just listen without giving advice or being a problem-solver? Or maybe your partner prefers to be given physical comfort, without you being verbally responsive at all?

Everyone defines support in his or her own way when feeling overwhelmed, needy, troubled or in a crisis. So the question is: What do you prefer? And what does your partner prefer? Here are some of the more common definitions of emotional support that you can give to each other. *Neither is better nor worse than the other!* For each of us it is a matter of pure preference.

• *Some simply like being left alone.* I put this one first because this is how in my marriage I usually prefer to be supported, especially when I am feeling overwhelmed. It is important that I have at least a half-hour or so to sort things out privately, and then have the option of talking things over with my wife after I have gotten all I need out of my own solitude.

• *Some people prefer being held or comforted* and like not to talk, but just to be soothed on a feeling level or to be listened to without response.

• *Others prefer having their partners take charge of the situation*, or at least become actively involved. Looking to your counterpart to talk things over with, to fact-find or possibly even to act as a devil's advocate works quite well for many people.

• *And yes, for some, simply talking the situation over is still the best possible approach.* However, check with your partner what role you are best to take in that conversation. Your partner may want to talk it out, or simply monologue — but may *not* appreciate your (however well-intentioned) attempts to give advice or problem solve. An empathetic listening ear may be your best response.

• *It's important also to recognize — and this makes it even more complicated — that some people prefer different things at different times.*

• Most importantly, when one of you is upset: *Talk about how you feel when you're ready, but at the very least, ask for what you want!* Don't assume that your partner should know automatically. Sometimes we have mixed emotions when we are feeling troubled. But as in all areas of your relationship, communicating about these things will make the critical difference. Remember, it is perfectly fine to be confused. You might say "I'm so upset now I don't know how I feel" or "I might want you to help me later, but I don't know what I need yet." That's especially important if you just need some time to sort things out.

• *Don't misinterpret a request to be left alone as a rejection or an attempt to shut you out.* This may merely be your partner's way of coping with the situation. If you are willing to step back when your partner wants some space, this is merely being respectful of your partner's needs. On the other hand, if you feel threatened by being shut out, you may be misinterpreting a mere request for solitude as a rejection. In all likelihood, it is not that at all and you will be as close as ever, if only you can give your partner the necessary time and space.

• *Don't judge what you prefer with respect to your own needs as better or worse than other things.* We become the people we are through trial and error. Most of our styles and preferences develop because we find what really works for us and we then make choices for our own reasons and in our own ways.

• *Think about, and then talk about, how you each like to be supported* at those times when support is really what you need from your partner. An excellent strategy for doing this is to write it out in detail, under the heading: *"Instructions for Supporting Me When I Need It the Most."* Then make copies of what you have written; and exchange your lists of "instructions." You can also give each other copies at times when the partner who needs *to do* the supporting forgets. I never cease to be amazed at how many needless arguments and false assumptions this type of clarification can prevent! Of course, whatever you put on your written instruction list is subject to change; and it's a good idea to also agree that verbal instructions specific to the moment take precedence over your lists. But most of the battle here is in realizing how we are different in this respect.

Honoring Your Differences

To paraphrase Christine in the last chapter: "If two people agree on everything, are both people necessary?"

How you give support to each other *is merely one example* of how you may be opposite, and where that opposite nature can be wreaking havoc in your relationship. Most couples can name several opposites: neatness versus sloppiness; extroversion versus introversion; being high-strung versus laid-back. I'm sure you have something in mind that's specific to you. It is true in some respects that opposites attract. But *those areas where you are opposite generally need a bit more work to insure that they don't destroy you!*

Look at it this way: To the extent that you see things from an opposite standpoint, *you always have a choice.* You can allow those areas where you are opposite to be a constant and nagging *source of trouble* for you by demanding that your partner be just like you; or you can let them serve as some of your greatest strengths, by allowing yourselves to have a much greater perspective as a *team* than you could possibly ever have on your own!

The choice is yours. Couples who can use those *opposite characteristics to their own advantage operate with four eyes and four ears, rather than canceling each other out.* And canceling is often the result when there is perpetual conflict. *But getting this to work fully to your advantage can present a challenge.*

▪ Here's an exercise to help you deal with the opposites in your relationship. Think about and/or discuss all of the ways in which you are opposites. Next, make a list of all those opposite traits or habits that you are able to recognize. Then, review your list, assigning a plus (+) or a minus (-) next to each item you have identified to *indicate whether your opposite trait is a positive or negative factor in your relationship.* Couples who take the time to do this thoroughly are usually quite surprised to find that most of their opposite traits in some way serve them! (Obvious examples: One loves to cook; the other hates to (but loves to eat); one is a good money manager, the other is inept at handling finances; one is a very strict parent, the other is quite liberal.)

John and Sheila, demonstrate a slightly less obvious example. John's idea of a vacation is to go someplace warm, and lie on the beach or at a pool. Sheila loves vacations where there is lots to do and see. In fact the more her schedule is crammed with activities when she is away, the better. They fought so bitterly about their vacations that they spent several years not going away at all, despite the fact that they could well afford to. Their solution: vacations where each could do what he or she wanted. Sheila found a few "best of" hand-picked activities John would enjoy, so he wanted to join her. John could spend the vast majority of his time during the day doing what he wanted — while Sheila was partaking of the rest of the sights. They both believe that this simple effort changed the entire climate of their relationship by defusing a chronic issue.

Now take a look at each item that you have identified as negative and discuss a strategy to use that opposite trait to your advantage.

No matter how opposite you may be, there has got to be some overlap. *Consider that overlap as the strength that can help you to convert those parallel tracks to ones that are more convergent!* Couples who work hard on doing this are usually delighted to find that they can make a great team (even though it may have been one in hiding) simply because they learned to complement one another.

Getting Past Your Issues

With very few exceptions, two people in a relationship can learn how to communicate well — *but they must want to and then work at it together!* This can put that crucial ingredient I call *comfort* truly within your reach. By keeping in mind some of these points (in addition to those I discussed in this and the previous chapter) regarding communication, you and your partner together should be able to weather practically any issue, problem or crisis.

What follows are some principles and strategies for making your new life together really work this time. You'll note that I've included my rating system to show you how important they are to your future as a couple:

> ★ — May be irrelevant in some relationships, but in others it can have a definite effect on your quality of life together.

> ★★ — When this is not working, you relationship will probably be feeling a good bit of stress.

> ★★★ — Most couples find that when this goes awry, their relationship is on a slippery slope.

> ★★★★ — It is of make-or-break importance.

So here they are in order of their increasing importance to your staying together, beginning with one-star items and working up to four-stars:

• *Be careful about what you share with your family and friends concerning your relationship.* Although discussing your relationship and its issues with outsiders can feel quite good when you are upset, you may regret it later when things get patched up, but those you talked to still remember that negative spin and may harbor negative feelings toward your partner for which you long forgave him/her. So just in case you ever do share the problem, be sure to share the resolution as well — before any consequences occur. (★)

• *Learn to take risks with each other.* Never underestimate the power of risk taking. Is there some issue that may be bothering your partner? Or something that's been bothering you, which you are reluctant to bring up? A part of risk taking is making your needs known. Often this means being vulnerable. Each time you open that channel, the momentum shifts positively. Ultimately, those risks will make your relationship deeper, closer and more enjoyable for both of you. Caution: I would also be remiss not to remind you that *sharing certain things with your partner can also signal the kiss of death!* In confessing an affair, for example (as discussed in chapter 5), or being brutally or meanly "honest" about something *un*important, the negative impact of your message can far outweigh the importance of it. Only you can weigh what is appropriate in your own situation, but err in the direction of sharing those things (such as your sexual desires, what makes you sad, or other areas of vulnerability) that have the power of bringing you closer by putting more of the intimacy ingredient into your relationship. When in doubt, think through the consequences of saying it versus not saying it. Never forget this: *You can always share "it" later, but once it's said, you can't unsay it.* (★)

• *Remember,* how *you say something is usually way more important in the end than* what *you say!* The message could be right, but your tone could totally negate the message you are trying to send. If you see this happening, realize that you are not getting anywhere and remember — *for the sake of both of you — back off!* (★★)

Shelly: "We worked to make *our home a safe haven* for each other instead of a hostile environment. Once we could do this together — as a team — it all fell into place."

• *Work hard on your ability to* empathize *with each other.* Empathizing does *not* mean agreeing, but simply *understanding* how your partner feels. Healthy relationships have plenty of room for disagreement, but much less for lack of empathy. If you are having difficulty empathizing — that is, seeing each other's perspective or point of view, *try trading places* by doing this exercise: First, simply arrive at an agreement as to *what the problem issue is.* (For example: "We disagree on whether and how to discipline our teenage son. She is too strict/He is too lenient.") Next, *switch roles.* Assume the role of your partner, and let your partner take on your role. Then resume your discussion of that same issue with the roles switched. When you do this exercise, remember one very important point. *Play the role as you see each other in that situation where you're having difficulty.* Use this as a source of information so that you can understand just what your partner's frame of reference or point of view may be when he or she reacts to you in a way that pushes your buttons. Many couples find trading places or reversing roles to be a very powerful strategy. It can be used almost anytime you find yourselves at an impasse. I cannot think of a time when it is not in the best interests of both of you to — at the very least — *have a solid awareness of each other's needs, desires and feelings.* What you then do with that information is up to you. (★★)

Patricia: "I used to take things so personally. After all, what could be more personal than your marriage? I learned to *check out what my husband meant* by certain things he would say. As a result now I rarely get upset anymore."

• *A full-blown argument where nobody wins cannot happen unless both of you collaborate to make it happen.* If your partner is raising his or her voice, you lower yours. Don't believe that by being the pacifist you are wimping out. When one of you is so angry that you are about to say or do something you will regret, call a timeout and remove yourself temporarily from the situation. Remember that anger and hurt usually come about in stages, which can quickly accelerate — *and then, take on that dreaded life of its own.* Never let it get so vicious that you burn bridges. The earlier you can stop it in its tracks, the better. Important: *Be sure to revisit the conflict when you can concentrate on a solution without being overwhelmed by emotions.* (★★★)

Jerry: "I no longer consider *compromising* a sign of weakness (or a 'birthright' that my partner compromise)."

• *Avoiding contentious issues doesn't work either.* If your anger tends to get bigger than the problem or issue you're angry about, it can be quite tempting to try to avoid the issue altogether. This is like refusing to see the proverbial "elephant in the room." Sooner or later — I guarantee you — that strategy will fail! Instead, move learning to deal with your anger — *before it gets out of control* — to the top of the list. (★★★)

Sara: "Instead of trying to avoid the inevitable little crises that come up, I learned to confront them *with my partner* and not blame him for them."

- *Insisting that you be right, or that you have the last word is rarely compatible with what's in your best interest as a couple.* This will not get you that all-important *win-win* you are seeking. In my office, on the radio and in seminars over a period of many years I have spoken to many people who saw their — perhaps potentially great — relationship fizzle out because they treated it as a contest. They concentrated so much on winning the battles that they lost the war. So to the extent that you have to battle at all, choose those battles wisely and sparingly. When in doubt, err in the direction of giving in — which is almost always the direction that will get you more (and lasting) peace. (★★★)

Phillip: "I had a lot of *regrets.* Once I decided to *let them go* everything changed."

- *Set time aside to talk regularly.* Turn off the television and remove any other distractions, even if it is just for ten or fifteen minutes. *I have yet to meet a couple that could not do this if they really tried!* And I have known some very busy couples. The best strategy is to plan regular talks — and even "meetings" — where you can work things out that tend to be ignored or neglected in favor of more pressing priorities during the rest of the week. Some of the biggest and most destructive relationship issues are those that build up slowly because they are not dealt with while they are small. On the other hand, *too much intensity* — too many or endless meetings — can also be a destructive thing. Be sensitive to what works in your situation. Keep a healthy balance between keeping open the lines of communication, in order to be current with each other, and putting yourselves under too much scrutiny. It has been said that "marriages are rarely destroyed as much by the boulders in life, as by the pebbles." (★★★)

- *Some couples when reconciling find that once they are back together, they don't want to address the reasons they split in the first place.* As one who is trying to help them to get past those issues that prevent their healing permanently, that has often puzzled me. But ironically, I have found that many couples have actually been able to sweep old hurts under the rug, and avoid dealing with them at all — *ever.* If you can do this *without* ever dredging those things up, you are unusual indeed. But so be it. However, if any of those painful issues do come up again — even one time — you *know that your strategy of avoidance is not working!* Then do whatever it takes to work it through in order to really get past it. Otherwise, you are almost certain to pay the piper later — and at a high interest rate! (★★★)

Marie: "We both did a lot of acting out — I did by diverting too much attention to the kids; my husband did by diverting too much attention to work. By realizing we were *both* doing that we stopped blaming each other."

• *Learn to forgive!* I cannot stress this enough. No matter what it is that you may be angry about, *by refusing to truly forgive* — regardless of the issue — *chances are your relationship will not last.* Forgiving does not necessarily mean forgetting, but it means that you agree to let go of the anger and pain you feel toward your partner. Then you can transform your open wound to a benign scar. And watch out for those *"wildcards."* For example, if one of you did something that the other considered at the time to be unforgivable (such as having an affair or squandering an amount of money you couldn't afford to lose), bringing up that "wildcard" when you are discussing or arguing about an *unrelated* issue will *create a climate from which your relationship ultimately will not survive.* So once you have resolved an issue as best you can, *do whatever it takes to let go of it!* Some couples even find it helpful to establish a twenty-four hour, forty-eight hour, or one-week rule. That is, if it is not brought up again *within that period of time* after you have declared it resolved, *it is dead forever* — and thus totally out of bounds. Digging up old unresolved matters to justify your current dissatisfaction is one way your relationship may have gotten into trouble in the first place. Couples who are most likely to stay together are those who allow healing to occur, no matter how delicate the situation, *by never pulling the scab off of old wounds.* (★★★★)

Sonny: "I acknowledged my role in my wife's affair, and was then able *to forgive her.* It's been a year now, and I haven't looked back."

If you are still finding it difficult to get beyond an issue — to resolve it permanently, then it's time to look at what *purpose* that issue is serving. In other words, what's in it for you to keep it alive? Here are some questions to ask yourselves and some strategies for answering them —

again in order of their increasing importance to staying together, beginning with one-star items, working up to four-stars:

• Is the issue keeping you and your partner sufficiently distant so that you feel less *vulnerable*? If so, explore — hopefully together, but at least by yourself — what being vulnerable in this relationship really means to you. What are you really afraid of? What are you willing to do in order to assure each other that the climate is now safe? (★)

• *Try brainstorming solutions together to come up with as many ideas as possible* — allowing that some of them may even be laughably absurd. But brainstorming is a great way to tap into your collective creativity. Then talk through every potential solution you come up with. Brainstorming is a well-established problem-solving device used in business and other organizations to create fresh options. If done in the right spirit, it can do wonders for your relationship as well. Some couples find that brainstorming can be fun, since any crazy idea is allowed, without criticism. A great bonus of this technique is that it helps you to see yourselves on the *same team*, rather than as opponents. Couples who continue who see themselves as *teammates* — even when things get rough — can use that synergy they create to certainly resolve, and often to *permanently obliterate* almost any issue. (★)

• *Avoid the tendency to nitpick.* Nitpicking (at each other especially regarding small insignificant things that are overblown) is usually analogous to the "fumes" resulting from a much bigger issue that lurks somewhere slightly under the surface. You may be trying (in vain) to avoid that larger issue; but if you look for it with the intention to decimate it, chances are you will be successful with the symptom (nitpicking) *and* the real issue. (★★)

• *Put humor into your interactions.* Learn to laugh at your issues. Life is way easier and much more fun if you can loosen up together. Not only that, but humor can turn logic upside down. And that's a wonderful way to diffuse tension. By making fun of yourselves and your quirks in a lighthearted way, you can remove the stinger from almost any difficult or seemingly impossible situation. And there's probably no better way to cut a conflict down to size. You may choose to take your relationship very seriously, *but don't take yourselves too seriously!* (★★)

• *If your relationship has been suffering from a passion deficiency* (which may or may not be related to other issues), use those commu-nication/problem-solving strategies and techniques to explore what specifically the underlying problem may be, what it is that would be satisfactory to both of you, and how to go about getting there. In the area of passion, first be clear about what is *acceptable*, before exploring what may be great. *Great sex will elude you until you have established a sex life that is* good enough. So take it in *small steps*. There are many proven strategies that can help you to first to establish (or re-establish) a satisfactory sex life; and then to enhance the passion you feel toward each other. They are beyond the scope of this book. Some excellent books and resources that do this important subject justice can be found in the Appendix. (★★★)

Chris: "We found a way to *revive the early feelings of romance* that got us together in the first place. I would never let any problem take that away from us again!"

• *Are your efforts to stay together merely a way of kidding yourselves?* Are you trying to reconcile out of *desperation?* (That's an idea that just about *never* works in the long run.) If so, expect that your relief from the desperation will unfortunately be short lived, and so will your reconciliation! Stop and ask yourself what is the reality here? Is it possible that you *wish* you truly wanted the relationship to stay together, but you really don't? Whatever that truth is, face it head on. That truth will *ultimately* give you the answers you need. Turning your back on it will never serve you in the end. (★★★★)

• *Don't get sucked in to that "Soul Mate Syndrome"!* Remember, nobody's needs are *one-hundred percent* fulfilled all of the time. Perfection is *not* an option (for this partner *or* any subsequent one). Having *absolutely everything* you want or *all* of your needs fulfilled by one person is about as likely as the two of you having identical genes! And remember that the longest-lasting and best relationships are those that are grounded in the pillar I call *comfort*. Sure, there can be that other pillar — *passion* — as well, with all those deliciously intense, positive, romantic, and sexy feelings. But as important as passion may be to you, it is rarely enough to sustain a full-time long-term relationship! Your ability to support one another day-to-day, and to resolve your conflicts together will prove to be a much more accurate predictor of whether you will survive as a couple than anything else. (★★★★)

• *Do you have an especially difficult, long-standing, or tricky issue that you know will re-surface or continue to wreak havoc on you, your partner, and your relationship?* If so, make a commitment not only to resolve it, but to *obliterate* it. That is, to use every possible strategy available to you (including couples' therapy) to address it in a way that makes it most unlikely ever again to resurface. Just like a drop of ink in a flask of water can darken all the water in that flask, that thorny issue (for example, a past affair, the refusal to have children, the in-laws, the bankruptcy, the big lie, the gambling addiction) can do the same to darken all areas of your relationship. Don't give up on that problem until the situation has changed; you have been able to accept it or, at the very least, understand it so that it no longer tears you apart. Getting your toughest issues to an optimal win-win solution only takes practice and the determination of both of you. *Accept nothing less!* (★★★★)

Lorne: "Whenever I would make a concession to my partner, I would begin to resent her for it. I finally realized that this was inconsistent with finding *a win-win solution.*"

Some Additional Perspectives on Keeping Your Relationship Together

• Yes, be open and honest with one another, but not in a way that in the name of "honesty" it becomes more of a source of hurt to your partner than a source of intimacy. (★★★)

• Let your partner pursue what is important to him or her and make an agreement that both of you will do that for each other. This includes allowing each other some space and privacy. Also, be sensitive to your partner's need to be alone. If there is one ingredient present in the happiest couples I know, it is this form of mutual support. (★★★)

• Building trust is crucial. But remember, building trust and increasing intimacy is a lifelong, ongoing process. (★★★)

• Separate from anyone who is interfering in your relationship, such as friends, family members, or in-laws. This separation does not have to be a physical one or a permanent one. But it should be enough of *an emotional one* so that you can be present for each other without outside interference. (★★)

• Remember, that with respect to relationships, there is really no such thing as genuinely "unconditional love." In fact, *love is conditional based not on who you are but on what you do.* In other words, no matter how unconditional your love for your partner may feel, there is always something he or she could do to put that love in doubt (and vise versa)! Who you *are* cannot be changed; what you *do* can. Taking each other for granted simply means forgetting this very important truth about relationships. (★★★★)

This Could Be an Ongoing Process

The strategies in this chapter have been designed to take you another major step past your ambivalence. They are meant for you to apply to your unique situation. However, if after reading this chapter you are feeling ambivalent again, or if these strategies remind you of taking bad-tasting medicine (or simply make you cringe), *then maybe you are still in the decision-making process.* If that's the case, go back to the appropriate sections of Part Two. You may also find it helpful to read ahead. Chapter 7 will give you a peek at the single life.

7

NO, IT CAN'T BE SAVED
MAXIMIZING YOUR NEW SINGLE-AGAIN LIFE

~

'Tis better to have loved and lost, than never to have loved at all.
— Alfred, Lord Tennyson

A caller to my radio program once told me that her newfound definition of wisdom was "I now know that I won't die just because we broke up." Another caller followed up with something that, in my opinion, was just as wise: "When someone dumps me, she has actually done me a favor. In spite of my bruised ego, I can now get on with my life without this person who took up my precious time and didn't care a lick about my feelings."

The assumption of this chapter is that your relationship has ended — *run its course*. That decision was made either *by* you, *for* you (that is by your partner), or you and your partner arrived at a *mutual* agreement that it was time to move on. And even if that is not the case, this chapter can serve as a frame of reference. It explores life in the aftermath of your relationship, along with some of the issues of being single once again, and some strategies for addressing those issues. Although we will look at a few of the aspects of becoming involved with your *next* partner, a far more powerful master strategy for you right now is to *become emotionally free*. That way you will now replace the relationship you are leaving with the freedom either to remain on your own, *or* to become involved once again — but only when you are ready. *Then your next relationship will be a choice, not a necessity for happiness.*

Single Phobia
I have talked to scores of people over the years that have stayed in horrendous and even abusive relationships simply out of the fear (of almost phobic proportions) of being single. In fact, my expression "single phobia" can very accurately describe why some allow themselves to stay

in such bad relationships. The fear of financial ruin, never finding another partner, the shame of being an outcast, disappointing other people, or the loss of social status are just a few reasons why so many thoroughly unfulfilling, stifling, and even life threatening relationships survive! This is why in chapter 4 I refused to judge negatively the tactics for leaving used by those who determined that their relationships must end — no matter how unconventional or politically incorrect they were. Furthermore, some of the *un*happiest people I have met throughout my career have been those in bad relationships with the "between a rock and a hard place" belief that life could never be anything short of horrible, if they were *not* involved with a partner. If this feels familiar to you, *by conquering your fears and insecurities regarding your life as a single, I can practically assure you that you will never again get into another relationship out of fear!* Additionally, I believe that if we suddenly found a cure for that single phobia (and put it in the water supply) that would cause people to stop being afraid to go it alone, and thus leave their bad and unfulfilling relationships, the current divorce rate would certainly skyrocket *temporarily*. But soon that divorce rate would dramatically and permanently drop to a much lower level than it has ever been — since those getting re-involved (either with an old partner or a new one) would then be doing it out of *desire* rather than fear!

When I wrote *The Art of Living Single* (Avon, 1990), I made it a point to ask every person I interviewed these two questions: "What is the *best advantage* you can tell me about being single?" and "What have you found to be the *worst disadvantage* of the single life?" You might want to think about this for a moment, and note how *you* would answer these questions.

Practically everyone I interviewed pointed to the awesome amount of *freedom and choice* that a single lifestyle provided them as being the best thing about single life. This response even came from people who swore that life as a single is something they would never ever choose in a thousand years! If you are wondering what consistently came up as the worst aspect of single life, it was those *feelings of loneliness and isolation* that are sometimes a by-product. In other words, choice and freedom and all the benefits of *healthy selfishness* are what you get with being single (if, of course, you can take advantage of them). But like practically everything else in life, there's a price, or a flip side. And for many, the downside of living single is those lonely feelings.

That is why it's important to know what those feelings really are and how to conquer them. Once you have learned *how to do that* and then learn *how to experience and enjoy your power and freedom to the fullest*, it will take a truly special person to get you to give your new lifestyle up in favor of another relationship. (And isn't "truly special" what you would really want your next partner to be?) So the first step toward this goal is to become comfortable outside of your relationship that has ended. For you, this could even mean acknowledging the *possibility* that your new lifestyle may be a permanent one. Once you have arrived at that degree of *acceptance,* whether or not to find a new relationship will become simply one more *choice* — but never an *obsession!*

Your New Single Life

What is it that most concerns or worries you about now becoming single? Here are some other answers to this question by a few people who were about to leave long-term relationships:

- "Telling my *relatives and friends,* and then having them judge me negatively and look at me as a fifth wheel or with pity."
- "Getting along *financially.*"
- "Realizing that no matter what comes up, *I have to face it myself.*"
- "I just wonder *what will become of me* — the uncertainty of the rest of my life is terrifying."
- "I fear meeting the characters that everyone tells me frequent every place *that single people go.*"
- "*Raising the children* alone."
- "I always considered divorced people *losers.* Now I guess that's what I am."
- "As bad as it always was, I could always turn to my partner in *times of crisis.* Who do I turn to now? Who would take care of me if I got sick?"
- "It wasn't all bad; there were lots of things that we enjoyed doing together. I guess I'll have to *give some things up,* or somehow learn to do them *alone.*"

How about *you? What is the issue (or issues) that worries you the most about your new life as a single?* Are there any statements that you tell yourself over and over again that translate to: "I *can't* do it, make it, or make it happily"? *If so, note it, and then let's confront that enemy head-on!* One way to do this is to pretend for a moment that *you can.* Make a list of things — perhaps twenty — that you would do differently with your life if you believed, with one hundred percent certainty, that you would not only *be able to survive,* but that you will *flourish* in your new life. Keep this list handy. It will become part of a larger strategy that will run through this entire chapter.

Here is another visualization exercise that you can try any time you are getting a bout of that "can't do" feeling:

> *Close your eyes and imagine that your life is working extremely well. Imagine that there's nothing about your life that you believe should be different. (Pause) Imagine that you have all the strength and support you could ever need to pull off the reasonable goals that you have chosen and will now be free to continue to choose for yourself. (Pause) Let yourself really feel this attitude becoming the dominant one for you. (Pause) Take some time to become aware of how different you feel when you empower yourself. (Pause) Be aware of what you would like to do with your newfound strength.* (Stay in this frame of mind for as long as you'd like. Make notes of what you have visualized, remembering that you can always come back here whenever you'd like to add to this experience and your notes about it.)

Some additional things you can put into your visualization:

> *Imagine that you have unlimited capabilities and are immune to all fear and anxiety. How will you now change your life? How will you then handle_____ differently?* (Plug in an issue you are now struggling with.)

Your Custom Survival Guide

I strongly suggest that you now start your own custom "Survival Guide." Your survival guide is a very personal resource that includes both your specific *issues* and the *solutions* that you arrive at as you transition to a new life. Consider your survival guide a *master list of personalized triggers* that you can pull whenever you need them (containing the very things you may not remember when you are in the heat of an issue). The lists you have already made in this chapter, along with your notes from the visualization, can be the start of your survival guide. Throughout this chapter I will suggest several more things that you can include in your custom survival guide.

One very powerful and effective strategy that you can use for just about any situation where you feel like that proverbial "duck out of water" is called the *act-as-if* technique (in other words, "fake it 'till you make it"). The visualization exercise in this chapter is a beginning part of this strategy. For example, *if you are feeling lonely, challenge yourself to act as if your life were full right now.* Then become aware of what you would be doing differently at this moment *if that were true* (and your life were now as full as you could possibly want it to be).

In fact, let's look at that question: "What is it that you are telling yourself you *cannot do now,* which you believe *would be possible* if you did not have — what you feel to be — a void in your life?" For example, if you are telling yourself, "Nothing is possible now," or, "I can't feel different now," your challenge is simply to *pretend that is not true.* You will be amazed at the strength that you can conjure up. By using the *act-as-if* technique, you are, in essence, *being a rational best friend to your emotional self* — and the best part is that there are no strings attached! For instance, if you are troubled by the prospect that you will never be in another relationship, think about *how you would live your life differently if you knew that you would be in an ideal relationship soon,* and had no worries about the prospect of remaining single until then. How would you be conducting yourself differently? Whatever you come up with is excellent material for your survival guide that you can draw upon whenever you need to.

While in the frame of mind where you are acting as if you have all the strength and wisdom you need to have, *make a to-do list that addresses all of the new obstacles in your life right now.* It could include finding a place to stay, getting legal consultation, telling certain people you have become separated, or dealing with financial matters. The fact is — *you know what they are.* If you find that you are putting off the prospect of looking at these items, issues, or challenges, face them head on. The strength to do so is there and you need only to acknowledge it.

Making the Transition

Several people whose marriages or long-term relationships had ended (by their own choice, their partner's, or mutual) somewhere between six months and two years ago were asked *what insight or revelation helped them most to make their transition?* All of them told me that they had, at the very least, some *initial* reservations about the breakup, but now see it as permanent and completely believe that it was the right thing.

- "Once I saw my *children would survive,* I knew I could."

- "The people I was most afraid would abandon me, or judge me harshly, didn't. But even more importantly was the realization that, just in case they do, I suppose I don't really need them anyway."

- "I was afraid I couldn't *resume my career*, but found that not to be the case. Had I known that, I would have left much earlier."

- "I realize that life doesn't give you happiness. It only gives you time to use it as best you can. *My marriage was absolutely* not *the best use of that precious time!*"

- "I was suffering from the 'I'm nothing without a man' syndrome. The surprise of my life was that once I left, *my self-esteem went way up!* I no longer feel that way and have a hard time realizing that I ever did."

- "I was afraid that I couldn't do with less money. I was truly surprised at *how unimportant money* became after the marriage ended."

- "I was always uncomfortable *doing things by myself*, and envisioned myself becoming a recluse. I took a few risks and saw that what I was thinking was a lot of nonsense."

- "I was feeling torn between the lifestyle of my marriage and the one of being single. Then it occurred to me that I really wanted my freedom, but was afraid to leave the nest. *Each day it gets easier.*"

- "I always relied on my spouse to help me with any conflicts that came up — to the point where I thought I couldn't face them alone. *Once I had no choice, I saw that I could face them even better.*"

- "I never thought that I was self-sufficient until I realized how self-sufficient I had to be in order to survive in my marriage. So the answer for me *was to not to sell myself short.*"

- "*The ball is now in my court* (not someone else's) to make the years ahead of me happy ones."

- "I stopped panicking every time I felt a little bit of regret. Once I realized that this was natural and did not mean that I had made a mistake, it was like someone turned the lights on."

- "I hate transitions. When I come home from a vacation, I want to unpack my bags immediately. *So I took great pains to make the transition from being part of a couple as short as possible.*"

No matter what lifestyle you prefer, *living in transition* could represent the *worst* of all possible worlds. For example, if you are avoiding the task of choosing a permanent and comfortable living space — one where you would be proud to invite friends (not necessarily elaborate or expensive, just one that feels permanent and reflects you) — managing your finances properly or making the most of your vacation time, *that avoidance may be your way of making the statement that your new lifestyle is only a temporary one.* And unfortunately I have seen people stay in that *transition frame of mind* for as long as a decade or more. In many cases, this even becomes symbolic of how to *avoid* doing what it takes to build a new life.

How might you be keeping yourself in that transition frame of mind? Is there something that you would really like to be doing, that you are putting off until you are in that proverbial *next relationship?* In other words, if you considered yourself *totally out of transition*, how would you change your life? Given the reality of your resources, if you are not living there now, *what would be your ideal living space?* Would you move, fix up, or redecorate your place to make it *your home?* (By that I mean *within* your means, but with a permanent feel to it, as opposed to a place you are merely staying temporarily.) Would you plan your finances *differently?* Would you make better use of your *vacation* time?

To stop living in transition involves little more than learning a new attitude — make your own version of the statement "I am now going to stop putting off being alive!" You will then be a major step closer to thinking of involvement in your next love relationship as a *bonus*, rather than as a *necessity* for long-term happiness.

Many years ago I was contacted by a cruise company to do a seminar for singles aboard a major ocean liner. The company that was sponsoring the cruise had to secure a certain number of cabins three or four months before the date the cruise was to leave. They told me initially that they were getting a lot of response to the singles cruise, but that the deposits were unusually slow coming in. About three months before it was to depart, I got a call telling me they had not received enough deposits to go ahead with the seminar cruise, so we agreed to cancel it. A month later, when it was too late to reverse our plans and go ahead with the seminar, I got another call from the seminar promoter telling me that the deposits had just started briskly flowing in! Alas, since enough spaces had not been reserved far enough ahead of time, the ocean liner had made other use of those cabins. What happened was that many of the single people who ultimately wanted to take this cruise were hesitant to make the commitment four months ahead of time. Many told the seminar promoter that they did not want to give their deposit too soon for fear they would meet someone in the meantime. (And if this were the case, they certainly would not want to go on a singles cruise!) That person they "feared" (or "hoped") to meet, of course, did not show up for most. Thus, when they were available for the cruise, it was too late. *This merely illustrates an all-too-prevalent attitude behind that tendency to live in transition.* In this case, planning ahead was felt as an admission of defeat. An agent for the cruise company said that he had never seen this phenomenon in any other kind of cruise he had planned. But in my experience of working with the issues of single people who see themselves as living in transition, I was not at all surprised.

Take a moment now to picture yourself as being totally through the transition. Think about what you would change in your life, and add whatever comes up for you to a new page in your survival guide. (For example, taking some social initiatives, having a party, working on your personal growth and spirituality, taking a vacation — with other single people, or even alone.) Use the act-as-if technique to *act as if your transition were over,* and see if you are able to look at things differently.

If you are still in your relationship, but *anticipating the transition,* be aware that the transition process generally involves two major stages:

- *Letting go* of your ended (or ending) relationship emotionally, as well as taking certain steps, such as saying all of the proverbial "goodbyes," moving out, and doing whatever else needs to be done to actually leave the relationship you are leaving; and

- *Building a new life,* which includes all of the things we have talked about in this section that go toward giving your new life the feeling of permanency.

This topic by itself could fill an entire book. (Some excellent books on this subject appear in the Bibliography.) But I have included some ideas and strategies for those times when you begin to experience *cravings,* either for what is now (or soon will be) your ex-partner, *or* for the lifestyle you are leaving.

It is important to allow yourself to mourn your ended relationship — even if you were the one who decided to leave. Mourning involves the acceptance and willingness to experience the often wide range of emotions and cravings that inevitably surface. Unfortunately (for when we are in pain), our *feelings* have "a mind of their own" and don't tend to follow in lock step what our *intellect* says they should. But there are ways to lessen their painful emotional impact. Sometimes it can make all of the difference in the world simply to talk to someone who could provide you with some much-needed support — *empathy* — at those times when you are feeling the brunt of the negative thoughts or feelings (such as guilt, sadness or anger). Emotions, no matter how strong, are transitory in nature (the nice ones, such as happiness and joy, as well as those that are painful), *and periods of upset will usually pass* (however temporarily) *in a matter of minutes if you let them run their course.* Friends or family members who can truly be empathetic toward you at those moments when you feel overcome by difficult feelings can be invaluable sources of support during this period. We will talk more about friendship and your support system later in the chapter.

It is wise to avoid making important decisions at times when you are feeling upset. For example, if you find yourself missing your ex, or being tempted to accept a job offer you ordinarily would not want just so you can move far away, acknowledge your feelings, but resist the urge to take immediate action. Don't jump to attempt a speedy reconciliation (that in the right frame of mind you would not even consider) just out of the pain of that moment. If in the end that is the right thing to do, it will become apparent. But *don't lose sight of long-term consequences merely to alleviate short-term pain.*

Here is an exercise that many have found to be extremely therapeutic. *Write a letter to your ex during one of those times of craving,* saying (among other things) all of what you perhaps did not have the opportunity or the will to say until now. *Of course, that letter never needs to be mailed,* and if you do decide to mail it, wait a couple of days just to confirm that mailing it is what you *really* want to do. Writing it can greatly help to put your feelings into perspective and clarify them. I have often suggested to clients that they write a letter (again, not necessarily to be mailed) at any time they have an urge to say something to an ex where actually saying it might be something they would later regret. I have always found it interesting how the content of the letters change as one's healing process unfolds. You may want to keep copies of these letters in your survival guide as a strategy for tracking your progress. This is a very time-tested healing technique. The letters you write can take on many different tones:

- *A thank-you note:* "Thank you for letting me go." "Thank you for the years we shared together." "Thank you for helping me realize while I still have a lot of life to live that we are better off apart";
- *A note of anger* — just fill in the blanks;
- *An expression of grief:* "Even though I know we are not meant to be together, I still miss you very much and the good times we shared";
- *Guilt:* "I'm sorry for what you are going through now, but this is just the way it has to be."

One of the most common reasons people seek counseling or psychotherapy is to get help letting go *emotionally* of an ended relationship. You could be going through a period of extreme confusion, depression, anxiety and stress. But the right support — be it professional or otherwise — can turn that pain around very quickly, and rapidly bring that transition state of mind to a much-needed end.

Overcoming Loneliness

The many interviews I have done with the single people I referred to at the beginning of this chapter left absolutely no doubt that *the feelings of loneliness and isolation are what those who are single (or single again) most want to eliminate.* These feelings are, to some degree, inevitable, but not exclusively a part of the single life. My experience as a psychologist, combined with what I have learned writing two major relationship self-help books (one for singles and one for couples) taught me that *loneliness was just as prevalent for married couples as for singles.* But there is one major difference with couples that probably won't surprise you. Because they have a partner for which they can blame that "icky" feeling we know as loneliness, those who are part of a couple tend to call it something else, such as unfulfillment, neglect, or distance. It then follows that when there is no partner, you would have no alternative but to blame *yourself* (if anyone needs to be blamed at all) for that unhappiness you feel. It is that same feeling of emptiness only with a different label.

I find it important to point this out, mainly for you to keep in mind that the *cure for loneliness is not merely putting another love relationship into your life.* As we discussed in chapter 4, rebound relationships rarely amount to much more than *temporary solutions* for immediate and acute pain. (Some people even rebound into *inappropriate* new relationships, not only as a means to emotionally ease away from the previous one, but out of so much anger, that they want to inflict pain on the ex, or even to hurt that *new* person — often unwittingly or unconsciously — in order to compensate and place blame for the pain they feel.) But remember, while you're involved in a rebound relationship, it can feel very much like "true love."

Low commitment, transitional relationships are another matter. They can be great sources for company, fun, learning about yourself in this new era of your life as a new single beginning to date again, and yes, even sex. But to the degree you are still in transition emotionally, further involvement becomes a rebound relationship.

The *best solution* to loneliness is first to recognize and then change the attitudes that produce your lonely feelings. They include:

- The notion that the whole world is having a party to which you are not invited;
- The idea that you are trapped in this horrendous lifestyle with no way out;
- The belief that you are undesirable or unlovable. Perhaps you tell yourself some variation of, "If I weren't unlovable, I'd be happily in an *ideal* relationship right now"; or
- *The attitude* — however strong it may be — that you can *never be happy* until you are finally in that proverbial "ideal relationship."

To the extent that these (or your own unique version of them) are your attitudes and beliefs (and thus what you tell yourself), being alone at certain times will *feel like* isolation and loneliness, rather than what it *could be* — the very nourishing feeling of *solitude*. Solitude and loneliness are two very different ways you can choose to look upon being alone. One defines your *aloneness* in positive terms; the other defines it negatively. At the very least, being able to experience your aloneness as the positive and *self-nourishing* feeling of solitude will make your life as a single-again person tolerable. *At best, you will discover* (or perhaps *rediscover) solitude to be profoundly enjoyable and fulfilling!*

If weekends and holidays are the most difficult times for you to cope, the reality is that *they are little more than other days of the week or year.* But we are certainly capable of hanging additional meanings on to them! And these meanings are perfectly fine, when they add to your *happiness.* But when they add to your pain, that's another matter. Many folks compare the circumstances of their life *right now* (which may temporarily leave something to be desired) with a similar occasion that possibly took place at a much better time. I hear this quite frequently in my practice, particularly around Christmas time. In fact, holiday stress has become a cottage industry and a part of the American fabric. And all of these universal holiday issues center around the expectations you put on them. To understand the attitude behind expectations about times such as Christmas, New Year's Eve, Valentine's Day, and other holidays that are important to you — even your birthday or Saturday night — consider that there was never a better application to the adage offered by President Roosevelt during the Great Depression of the 1930s: "the only thing we have to fear is fear itself." It is so easy to fear being alone on these occasions that sometimes it's hard to remember that as fast as they come, they are over. So first, it is important to remind yourself that whatever the occasion is that you may be dreading, *it will soon pass.* Then, instead of fearing it, you can definitely choose to *face it head on*. If New Year's Eve has always been a night that you think of as being with someone special, and this year — whether you like it or not — it looks as if you are going to be alone, don't panic or scramble for some activity that you would really rather not do in the first place. Instead, consider using the occasion to prove to yourself once and for all that *you can stand being alone*. (And that furthermore, you not only can *handle the fear, but you can permanently obliterate it*.) One strategy is *to choose* the option of staying home. Then plan for yourself an ideal day or evening. You may be shocked to find that you are enjoying the occasion! In your case, this could even be an ultimate test in enjoying your solitude. Rent a movie, cook or order your favorite dinner, open a bottle of champagne to celebrate, or whatever it is that you would really enjoy doing with the *always-available resource of your own company*. I am certainly not going to try to convince you that this is going to be the best (or even one of the better) New Year's, Christmas, or birthday of your life, but I can practically guarantee that you will be quite unlikely to again have that *dire fear* of being alone during the occasions that so many single people dread.

Let me suggest that you now add to your survival guide some ideas you may wish to explore, that might even serve *two* purposes at the same time, providing you with the evidence that you can *face your fear;* and that you can *enjoy your own company* (even when being alone is not your first choice).

Maximizing Your Freedom, Aloneness, and Solitude
Once you learn to maximize the freedom that is now (or soon will be) yours to enjoy, I believe you will consider it one of life's greatest gifts. So here are some attitudes you can adopt to help you do just that. Those for whom "singlehood" tends to work — even if it is just for a short period of time in between relationships — seem to have these attitudes in common:

• Instead of defining quality time only as time spent with *other people*, you can learn to not only truly cherish your own company, but become fiercely protective of it. Develop interests that you can enjoy alone. *Make a strong, conscious effort to stop considering solitary activity as merely a consolation prize.* After all, when you get into a love relationship, aren't you in essence asking someone else to enjoy or love your company? Why shouldn't *you?*

• *You have a right to your own solitude.* Most people would not even think of telling someone who invited them out, "I'd rather spend some time alone today." Usually an "acceptable" excuse has you doing something with *another person.* Think about that. For many, the only acceptable excuse that involves being alone is to be sick! Some time ago I was at a conference in New York City where I gave several presentations and had a grueling day that included a number of very long meetings and constant stimulation. My colleagues planned dinner together for our two-hour break, and assumed that I was coming along. Instead, I told them that I had other plans and I would see them at our meeting later that evening. In fact, my plan was to take a magazine, go to a nice restaurant, relax, and have a quiet dinner by myself. After all, I had been talking all day, and there was still more to do after dinner. Well, guess what? With over 20,000 restaurants in New York City, this group of people walked right into the one where I was sitting, peacefully reading my magazine! "What's wrong?" they asked. "We thought you had plans."

"Yes, I do. My plans are to have a nice quiet dinner alone." I certainly acted as though there was nothing wrong with it, but I still got a lot of funny looks. After I gave my explanation, they understood. Later on, a few even confided to me that they, too, would have rather had a quiet dinner that night, but felt obligated, and were afraid of seeming aloof or offending their colleagues. Practically all of the *single* people that I have talked to have anecdotes like this where they felt a need to make excuses. So never feel defensive about your *right* to be alone.

• *Many wonderful and nourishing things can be done in solitude.* Many who re-enter single life after years of being part of a couple need to be reminded of that. Some of what we pursue in private can touch other people's lives. Other things are merely private pursuits — in some cases, even private passions — that can be infinitely rewarding when we allow ourselves to enjoy them. Just taking the opportunity to think and create can make our own company exhilarating. Feel free to listen to music (there's no reason why you can't enjoy a concert or a night at the opera by yourself), visit museums, galleries, exhibitions, sporting events, or engage in a visual experience of something that you enjoy, such as photography or working on photo albums. If you are someone who likes to read, every moment you are alone can be a chance to indulge in that pursuit. Some people enjoy gardening, playing with a pet, organizing a living arrangement, exercising, getting out into nature or traveling. Meditating or just thinking, fantasizing, participating in any creative or spiritual activity, writing, drawing, or taking a course in something that you would like to learn are just a few of the infinite number of things that you might indulge in on your own.

Begin another list for your survival guide of *things that you could enjoy alone* (which you might not think of doing during those times when you are feeling lonely — especially if you are overwhelmed by emotions). Think about your hobbies and avocations, what you would really *like* to do with your leisure time that you aren't doing or have been putting off. (This may include items that you did not have time to do as part of a couple.) It is a truism that one universal advantage to being out of a relationship is that you gain *a great gift of time*. But that time is a *gift* only if you use it to serve yourself.

If you believe that there are many things you would like to do that require a partner in order for you to enjoy them, I urge you to make another long list (at least twenty) of answers to this question: "If I had an ideal companion right now, I would _____." If that's how you feel, go ahead and make that list right now.

Finished? OK, now go through your list and identify which things *you are denying yourself* in the name of waiting for that next relationship. Which of the items that you listed *truly* requires a partner? Which of them *can* become a part of your life right now by either doing them alone or with a platonic friend of either sex? You will find that most — although not all — probably can. In other words, you will find that *there is little reason to put your life on hold until your next relationship, once you discover all that is possible to do on your own.*

Your Support System

I have long noticed that those who consistently make their single lives work well for them have one thing in common (besides enjoying *their own* solitude) — *they have a support system that they can count on.* Members of your support system can be friends, family members, colleagues, or certain professionals (such as an attorney, physician, or psychotherapist).

A good support system (with the exception of professionals whose services you pay for) is one where the support given is *mutual.* In other words, you can be the *giver* of support as well as the *receiver.* To avoid overwhelming your friends and even ruining friendships, it is important to give and listen, not just take and talk. This might sound obvious, but because they are often in so much pain and crisis, many who are going through divorce and separation unwittingly do just that — come across almost as "bottomless pits." Be conscious of the effect you may have on those people you rely on to support you; *be careful not to be too demanding.*

Having non-romantic friends of *both* sexes is ideal. Don't get caught in the trap of telling yourself you need a *love relationship* when what you can use even more right now is a *supportive friend*. Both are great, but they are not usually *interchangeable*. Organizations such as singles groups that have local meetings or sponsor trips are great places to meet new *non*-romantic friends, as well as folks looking for a more serious involvement.

Make a list of all the sources of support that are available to you — friends, family members, lawyers, financial advisers, various other professionals, formalized support groups, singles groups, seminars, self-help books and tapes, and virtually any other resource that could be helpful to you. Recognize those that are present in your life, and seek out others that are not. Make a special list of people who can be counted on during those times when you may be feeling the most isolated, or when you could use someone to talk to because you are having cravings for (and/or intense emotional reactions to) your ex, or your previous (coupled) lifestyle. *Be aware of who in your support system can be counted on — and for what* — during those times when you would prefer to have company, would like someone to reach out to, could use a sounding board, or would like some emotional support. *Keep this list handy in your survival guide.*

Your Next Relationship

I have done many, many lectures to groups of singles over the years. As critical as I think it is for me to talk about ways to maximize life as a single, I have found that the one thing audiences want to hear me talk about is anything I can tell them regarding *how to find their next love relationship*. The master dilemma facing those who are between relationships — once they have become comfortable with their new lifestyle — is the isolation sometimes felt as a result of not being part of a couple, versus the vulnerability that comes with the kind of love relationship that looks most desirable. While the topic of meeting that "special person" is beyond the scope of this book (refer to the appendix for other sources), here are a few points to consider when the time is right:

• *Avoid another unworkable relationship.* Be aware of *inappropriate partners* that may find you (and vice versa). They can include substance abusers, those who are physically abusive toward others (be aware of how they talk about their last relationship for clues), and people who cannot or will not truly commit. There are all types of individuals out there, including potential partners with whom you would thrive. The choice is yours.

• *Make sure that you are emotionally ready.* It bears repeating yet again that *rebound relationships rarely work long term.* This means that until you have genuinely let go of any lingering *preoccupation* with your last relationship, *you are probably not available* emotionally for lasting involvement. I believe that at any point in your life there is someone who will become attracted to you, and will need you more than you need them. Don't get "sucked into" a relationship *only* because of another's needs.

• *Focus on your core values.* Think about the traits, qualities and behaviors that you consider essential in a partner, then jot down your top five. Maybe you value honesty, trustworthiness, reliability, caring, and someone with a sense of humor. *Consider those non-sexy traits first. These are the ones that tend to remain constant as your new relationship progresses through its natural stages.* What is your prospective partner's relationship and family history? Do you share core values and beliefs? Do you feel safe around this person? Comfortable and at ease? Are you able to share true feelings? Can you talk openly about whatever matters to you? How do you feel about yourself (this is crucial) when you are with this person? Is there mutual respect? And yes, finally, is there a sufficient amount of passion, vis-à-vis romantic and sexual feelings, to say that this person could fulfill the passion requirement?

• *Pay close attention to how he or she talks about old relationships.* Is there a tendency to put down, blame or mistreat the ex? Remember, after what you have been through, you are looking for someone who has the maturity to take some responsibility for the issues that will arise. People who paint themselves as perfect and their ex as the constant villain don't usually meet that maturity standard.

• *Watch out for the "soul mate syndrome."* It is a mathematical truism that the more "perfect" a match you require, the fewer people will qualify, thus, the longer the wait. So when the time is right, beware of what may be a tendency to develop that "syndrome."

• *Be aware of whether a new involvement is really what you need or want!* Keep asking yourself, "If I had the ideal relationship now, what would I be doing differently?" Then pay attention to how your reaction to that question evolves.

Keep in mind that it's a rare person who would rather be single than in that elusive *ideal relationship.* This can be a nice time for you to date for fun, friendship, and simply to get back into the rhythm of dating again — if the opportunity is there. *But when will you be ready for a new long-term relationship?* Some say a year, but I hesitate to suggest a specific time. I say that when you are *at peace* with the reality that the right person may not show up for a long time, you are ready to start seriously looking. *Until then, if you make healing your first priority, you may never need this book again!*

Additional Strategies for Maximizing Your New Single-Again Life ("I'm All I've Got")

Keep adding to your survival guide as you become aware of new ideas, opportunities, challenges and affirmations. At some point in the not-too-distant future, these things will become second nature. *But in the meantime, take in all the help you need*:

• *Look at the affirmations that you have developed for yourself at times other than when you are upset.* For example, don't wait until those moments when you are overwhelmed with emotion to work on your loneliness problem. At those times usually the best you could hope for is to get past the immediate crisis (not unlike a couple trying to resolve an issue in the middle of an argument when both are angry). A time when you are happier — or at least in a neutral frame of mind — could be the best time to have a talk with the "you" that is sometimes susceptible to bouts of loneliness. *Think of your self-help literally as helping a friend who may have the same issues you do.* What makes it possible for you to help your friends is the fact that *you are feeling grounded,* while they are not. With some practice, you can take on the role of that *rational friend helping your emotional self.*

• *Write your affirmations (as well as other key parts of your survival guide) on 3x5 cards.* Keep the cards in your wallet or another handy place where they will be easy to reach for and refer to them routinely during those times when you need them the most (such as when you're feeling lonely). Using affirmations to counteract your self-defeating beliefs can almost always be a source of help to you, *but only if you remember to use them.* Some people find it even more helpful to attach the 3x5 cards containing their *most valuable affirmations* to their dashboards, refrigerator, bathroom mirror, or other places where they cannot help but see them — *regularly.* Eventually, these affirmations will become your new attitudes (and be as automatic as the self-defeating ones previously were).

Here are some additional ideas and affirmations. Use them as you see fit:

• "Even when I'm feeling lonely as a single, I acknowledge that there are people who are feeling a lot *more lonely within a relationship.* This pain I feel will soon pass if I allow it to."

- "I refuse to be afraid of *not* being part of a couple. *Instead, I transform that fear to challenge, enthusiasm, and freedom.* I acknowledge that no matter how well I do, being single will sometimes rattle me. But come to think of it, so did being in a relationship! Whose life is perfect anyway?"

- "I know the *only* one who can really make me happy is me, and I'll be as happy as I ultimately decide to be — *with or without a relationship.* It may be very difficult to find the *right* next relationship, but making new friends and enhancing existing friendships is easy, and can serve a lot of the same functions as a love relationship."

- "No one can now take away my freedom, my ability to come and go as I please, and my right to associate with anyone I find interesting."

- "I can now plan for my own future, career, lifestyle, etc., *without having to consult anyone.*"

- "'The grass is always greener on the other side of the fence' may be cliché, but there are unhappy couples who have just as much envy for me as I may have had for the happiest couple I know."

- "When I think others are looking at me unfavorably because of my single or divorced status I'll ask myself, 'Is this accurate, or am I merely putting myself down and imagining that others are also putting me down?'"

- "The more isolated I've become, the harder it may be to become free of that isolation. *But once I do, my choices are endless.*"

- "If I can enjoy and be nourished by my own solitude, *I can choose never to let anyone rob me of that solitude* again without providing fulfilling companionship in return."

- "Life as a single is never impossible or too hard, unless I define it that way."

Never believe the painful notion that you won't survive a life situation! You self-inflict emotional pain whenever you second guess or let yourself believe that things won't get better. This is an attitude that your rational side can now dispute when you need it to. You will survive! And — if you refuse to believe otherwise — you will be even happier, stronger and more fulfilled than ever!

I hope this chapter has helped to provide you with some strategies, tools, and strength to begin the journey of creating a new and fulfilling life, or gave you some insight as to what that journey would be like.

EPILOGUE

~

This is a book that, for many, will not end — at least not yet. Unlike most *business* decisions (once they're made, they're made) the decision as to whether to continue your *relationship* may need upgrading and re-evaluation many, many times.

Whether you've decided to stay, leave, or a creative combination of the two (such as living separately under the same roof), *I urge you to go back over the various strategies in this book often, especially when the issues you have already identified need more work or as new ones arise.*

The future is anyone's guess. The science of *predicting* the viability of relationships could not be less precise! As you heal from what may have been a major life crisis for you and those around you, *I urge you not to forget this period of time or the process you have undergone.* Please keep your notes from the various exercises for future reference. That way, you will be less likely to let the issues that brought you to this book repeat themselves.

If you're leaving, additionally please keep these things in mind:

• *Work hard to let go of your anger, guilt, blame, and all of the other negative feelings* that you feel toward your partner, yourself, anyone else involved (that other man or woman, the children, the in-laws, your partner's attorney or therapist, etc.) or anything else you associate with the relationship and/or its breakup. Those feelings won't do you any good, but will invariably eat away at you physically, emotionally, and spiritually to the extent that you continue to harbor them.

• If you have made a decision to leave (or one has been made for you) and it is *irreversible,* don't second-guess it! You now need to do whatever it takes to become free to *focus on the future.*

• As you move forward and straight ahead with your life, remember this — *it all happens for a purpose.* I can't prove that to you right now, but invariably time will.

• Whatever brought you to the point of leaving was probably a combination of many things that involve you, your partner, the interaction between the two of you, and all of the other people and circumstances in your lives. *Don't fool yourself into thinking that one simplistic reason was the cause of it all!* In all likelihood your breakup is the result of many factors — some may be glaring, while others are minor, but it is the complex *combination of them all* that did it.

• *Remember the good times as well as the bad.* The more realistic a view you can maintain of your ended relationship, the less your chances will be of repeating old patterns in the future.

If you are staying:
• Don't consider this chapter in your life to be over until you have in some way resolved *all the issues* that brought you to this crisis in the first place. Then once they are resolved, please — *let go of them forever!*

• Forgiving each other is a critical part of the letting go process. This means *no more grudges* about whatever you may have been angry about. Don't let your relationship be so fragile that anything that comes up has the potential of opening the Pandora's box you have worked so hard to close. *Instead, resolve to start again with a clean slate.*

• One way to avoid a relapse is to tackle any issue that surfaces while it is still small. *Never underestimate the importance of keeping things current!*

• Always give one another the benefit of doubt. And, don't be afraid to give in. Many *potential* issues are not worthy of the damage to your relationship that you can cause by dwelling on them. From now on, resolve to pick your battles wisely. Unless it is *truly* important, *drop it immediately!*

• *Long-term relationships are about much more than issues.* They are also about fun, play and lightness. Have regular dates together, plan fun activities (with your partner *alone,* as well as the kids), and do whatever it takes to keep your passion alive. These things are as important to the long-term health of your relationship as anything else.

If you are still in doubt and unable to come to a resolution using the strategies in this book, I suggest that you consult the Appendix, a therapist or clergyperson (by yourself or with your partner), or an attorney, and go back through the relevant chapters, *examining the questions that you will be asked in one form or another, regardless of who you consult.*

You have visualized being together; you have visualized being apart. No matter where things go from here, there is one thing that is crucial — *to live your life according to your own choices, sense of empowerment, and fulfillment.* I hope you can make that your definition of living life to the fullest.

APPENDIX
ADDITIONAL SOURCES OF HELP

<u>National Hotlines, Web Sites and Referral Sources</u>

✓ **Albert Ellis Institute**
1-212-535-0822, 45 E. 65ᵗʰ Street, New York, NY 10021
www.rebt.org
The Albert Ellis Institute has an excellent international referral list of mental health professionals who have been trained to use the cognitive behavioral approach (one that is compatible with the philosophy and strategies used in this book). They also publish a free catalog of books, tapes, seminars and other self-help material. Contact the Ellis Institute in New York for information regarding a center near you.

✓ **Alcoholics Anonymous**   www.alcoholics-anonymous.org

✓ **American Association for Marriage & Family Therapy**
www.therapistlocator.net
(A professional society of over 50,000 marriage and family therapists)

✓ **American Association of Sex Educators,
Counselors and Therapists**   www.aasect.org

✓ **American Bar Association** – Referral Service
www.abanet.org/referral

✓ **American Psychological Association** – Referral Service
1-800-964-2000, www.apa.org
(A professional society of over 150,000 psychologists)

✓ **National Association of Social Work**
www.naswdc.org/register
(A professional society of over 150,000 social workers)

✓ **National Hotline for Drug and Alcohol Information and
Referral Assistance**   1-800-662-HELP (4357)

✓ **National Domestic Violence Hotline**   1-800-799-7233

✓ **Parents Without Partners**   www.parentswithoutpartners.org

Tips on Professional Consultations

The best way to find a professional is through word-of-mouth, by someone you know who has successfully used that person and was satisfied with his/her services. The next best source is a referral from another professional familiar with his or her work. Using the yellow pages or other advertising sources is risky business, unless you can also get independent reference for the person you are about to consult with.

Legal Consultation

An attorney may be an important resource, especially if you are seriously considering divorce. If you are still in the process of deciding whether to stay or leave, make that clear to the attorney during your consultation. Elaine Smith, Esq., a Philadelphia attorney who specializes in divorce and other family matters — and whose legal perspectives appear throughout this book — says that you are better off consulting an attorney who will charge you an hourly fee for the consult, rather than one offering a free consultation. (Those who offer "free consultations" are often inclined to steer you in the direction of divorce. However this distinction may be less important if you have decided to go through with a divorce.) How do you find an attorney? Ask lots of people for names of recommended lawyers. Contact your local or state bar association for referrals. Or visit the web site of the American Bar Association (see listing above).

BIBLIOGRAPHY

Selected Books and Audiotapes by Dr. Broder

Books
The Art of Living Single. New York: Avon, 1990.
The Art of Staying Together. New York: Hyperion, 1993. New York: Avon, 1994.

Tapes
Help Yourself Audiotherapy Series. Philadelphia, PA: Media Psychology Associates, 2000 (rev.)

Topics Now Available:
- _Making Crucial Choices And Major Life Changes_
- _How To Manage Your Stress And Make It Work For You_
- _How To Develop Self-Confidence And A Positive Self-Image_: Permanently and Forever
- _How To Develop The Ingredients For Staying Together In Your Marriage Or Love Relationship_
- _How To Find A New Love Relationship_
- _How To Enhance Passion And Sexual Satisfaction In Your Relationship_
- _Overcoming Your Depression_
- _Overcoming Your Anxiety_
- _Overcoming Your Anger_
- _Can Your Relationship Be Saved? How To Make This Crucial Determination_
- _Letting Go Of Your Ended Love Relationship_: Overcoming the Pain Of a Breakup, Divorce, or Separation
- _The Single Life: How To Make It Work For You With Or Without A Relationship_

These and other materials by Dr. Broder are available at www.drmichaelbroder.com or by calling 1-888-650-TAPE (1-888-650-8273).

Author's address: Michael S. Broder, Ph.D., 255 S. 17th St., Suite 2900, Philadelphia, PA 19103.
Phone: 215-545-7000; Fax: 215-545-7014; E-mail: drbroder@aol.com

Other Books and Audiotapes

Being Single
McKinney-Hammond, M. *What to Do Until Love Finds You: Preparing Yourself for Your Perfect Mate.* Eugene, OR: Harvest House Publishers, 1997

How to be happy and single in the same breath, … practical as well as spiritual advice with a sense of humor.

St. Camille, M. and Moretti, L. *It's Okay To Be Single!* New York: It's Okay Publishing, 2000

A validation and affirmation for the single person. Full of great experiences, self-discovery and happiness.

Children and Divorce
MacGregor, C. *The Divorce Helpbook for Kids.* Atascadero, CA: Impact Publishers, 2001.

Warm, positive and supportive conversation with children of divorce by a talented writer who has "been there, done that." Covers the important bases in an easy-to-read, understanding, and informative style.

Ricci, I. *Mom's House, Dad's House: A Complete Guide for Parents Who Are Separated, Divorced, or Remarried* (Revised edition). New York: Simon & Schuster, 1997.

Guides separated, divorced, and remarried parents through the hassles and confusions of setting up a strong, working relationship with the ex-spouse in order to make two loving homes for the kids. Emotional and legal tools, as well as many reference materials and resources.

Rothchild, G. *Dear Mom and Dad: What Kids of Divorce Really Want to Say to Their Parents.* New York: Pocket Books, 1999.

A quick read that really helps to clarify the issues about children stuck in the middle of divorce. Simple, black-and-white, right-and-wrong style. Ten Commandments for Divorced Parents. (May be out of print, but available in some libraries or online resources.)

Stahl, P. *Parenting After Divorce: A Guide to Resolving Conflicts and Meeting Your Children's Needs.* Atascadero, California: Impact Publishers, 2000.

Gives parents supportive suggestions on how to put children's needs first. Detailed plans to help parents put self-interest aside and work cooperatively to meet child's needs.

Wallerstein, J., et al. *The Unexpected Legacy of Divorce.* New York: Hyperion, 2000.

Stories, statistics, and suggestions from a study of the outcomes of divorce. Features people of different ages and life stages, children of divorce, and families that stayed unhappily intact. Offers suggestions to strengthen marriages, practical how-to ideas, national policy initiatives.

Dealing with Divorce

Fisher, B. and Alberti, R. *Rebuilding: When Your Relationship Ends* (3rd edition). Atascadero, California: Impact Publishers, 1999.

Divorce recovery best-seller offers step-by-step process for putting one's life back together after ending a love relationship. Emphasizes emotional rebuilding and developing personal freedom before moving on to new relationships. There's help here for dumpees and dumpers.

Kranitz, M. *Getting Apart Together: The Couples' Guide to a Fair Divorce or Separation* (2nd edition). Atascadero, California: Impact Publishers, 2000.

Detailed guide to mediating a divorce settlement. Worksheets and specific plans help couples save a ton of money by working out the details of custody, property settlement, etc., before the lawyers get involved.

Krantzler, M. *The New Creative Divorce.* Holbrook, Massachusetts: Adams Media Corporation, 1999.

Update of the classic divorce guide. A new look at the process of breaking up.

Walton, B. *101 Little Instructions For Surviving Your Divorce: A No-Nonsense Guide to the Challenges at Hand.* Atascadero, California: Impact Publishers, 1999.

Concise advice from a practicing attorney who has handled hundreds of divorce cases. How to get through the process with fewest scars.

Webb, D. *50 Ways to Love Your Leaver: Getting on With Your Life After the Breakup.* Atascadero, California: Impact Publishers, 1999.

When you're left, you're likely to be devastated. Psychologist Webb presents personal experience and professional guidance to lead you through hurt and anger to forgiveness and beyond.

Titles by Impact Publishers, Inc. can be ordered through 1-800-246-7228 or www.impactpublishers.com.

Relationships

Ellis, A. and Crawford, T. *Making Intimate Connections: Seven Guidelines for Great Relationships and Better Communication.* Atascadero, California: Impact Publishers, 2000.

Most well-known and respected psychologist of our time presents relationship guidelines based on his rational therapy. Get your heads on straight and you'll get your relationship together.

Goulston, M. and Goldberg, P. *The 6 Secrets of a Lasting Relationship: How to Fall in Love Again-and Stay There.* New York: Putnam Publishing Group, 2001

Six relationship secrets make the acronym CREATE: chemistry, respect, enjoyment, acceptance, trust, and empathy. Strengthen the supporting structure in these overlapping areas and you'll restore passion, romance, mature love.

Sexuality

Barbach, L. *For Yourself: The Fulfillment of Female Sexuality.* New York: Signet, 2000.

State of the art strategies for understanding your own sexuality. A landmark in the literature of human sexuality. Clear factual advice for women. Simple, effective exercises.

Barbach, L. *For Each Other: Sharing Sexual Intimacy.* New York: Signet, 2001 (new edition).

Proven effective program for couples who wish to enhance sexual pleasure. Groundbreaking advice on physical and psychological dimensions by a pioneering expert in human sexuality.

Barbach, L. *Turn Ons. Pleasing Yourself While You Please Your Lover.* New York: Plume, 1998.

Erotic vignettes and simple suggestions for restoring romance and passion: sensory awakening, love, learning about each other, sex at home and elsewhere, spiritual sex, more.

McCarthy, B. and McCarthy E. *Sexual Awareness and Enhancing Sexual Pleasure.* New York: Carroll and Graf, 1998.

A comprehensive guide to effective techniques for improving a couple's sexual satisfaction.

Renshaw, D. *Seven Weeks to Better Sex,* New York: Dell, 1996.

Excellent self-help guide now out of print, but available in many libraries.

Zilbergeld, B. *The New Male Sexuality.* New York: Bantam Doubleday Dell, 1999.

Definitive guidebook for men and those who love them, offers readers up-to-date understanding of male sexual issues, and how to deal with them effectively.

Support Groups

Klein, L. *Support Group Sourcebook: What They Are, How You Can Find One, and How They Can Help You.* New York: John Wiley & Sons, 2000.

What support groups are, how they develop, and how they can function as a source of communal healing and strength. Moving insights, solid, expert advice and guidance, inspiring real-life stories. Practical guidelines on how to find, research, join, and participate in one, and how to form, sustain, and manage support groups of all types.

INDEX